"ARE YOU
LAS

"ARE YOU STRONG, LASS?"

Memoirs from a 1970s Yorkshire classroom

Kath Padgett

To whoever reads this book,
With Very Best Wishes
from Kath x

Scratching Shed Publishing Ltd

For my dear friend Judith,
always remembering the good times

Acknowledgements

MY thanks go to: David, for making me carry on searching for the right publisher; Janice, for reminding me of some anecdotes and reading my initial manuscript; Lynette for her unfailing encouragement and Mike for his patience – most of the time – and without whose computer skills, the entire book would have disappeared into cyberspace.

For reasons of privacy and respect, I have changed the names of the characters and altered identifying features.

Nevertheless, it remains an honest reflection of life as a young teacher in Yorkshire in the early 1970s; this is what it was really like.

Contents

Introduction

FOR as long as I can remember people said that I should write a book, mainly on the back of me constantly telling them that the stories I'd come across lent themselves to it.

I knew that lots of former teachers had put pen to paper and, having done a little research, I discovered that a large number of these accounts were based in the White Rose county and in North Yorkshire in particular.

Perhaps that should have discouraged me. The rural and leafy suburbs had not been my stamping ground early on in my career, quite the reverse in an inner-city deprived area where there was little evidence of angelic children doing sweet things presided over by endlessly patient teachers.

My story was more earthy, gritty, rude and heartbreaking, yet at the same time rewarding, challenging, life-changing and, every so often, vital.

Even in the raw, green early days as a newly qualified graduate teacher, I clung firmly onto the belief that it was necessary to reach out in teaching and attempt the impossible.

The majority of the kids did not always say or do what you wanted, none came from a privileged background, almost all were 'off the estate.'

In those first two years in the early 1970s, I laughed and cried almost in equal measure.

I encountered wonderful and inspirational people, many of whom turned out to be lifelong friends, and in addition to learning how to teach practically, I was taught how to learn.

I learned about real life, strength of character, tough love and the authentic things that really mattered, and of how to get by when you hadn't been dealt a great hand.

The pupils were amazing in so many ways and the teachers had to be even more so.

They survived on black humour to get through the toughest of situations, many of them outside the designated lessons.

We were driven on by the pupils who achieved wonderful things against all the odds.

Whenever I think back to my childhood, I recall that I had always wanted to teach. I used to create pretend forms and take fictional registers in hastily set-up classrooms in the front room.

There were no teachers in my immediate family and in retrospect, I think it was perhaps because I was an only child that I always craved the company of other children.

I was never lonely and had lots of friends but when they were not available, I invented my own.

At my first interview for my very first permanent job

after graduating, I was asked, "Are you strong, lass? You'll need to be to work in this school."

This question was put to me as I embarked upon my educational journey by Miss D. M. Brooke, the deputy head and was delivered in a steely and meaningful way which I came to realise was one of her trademarks.

I'd gained a modern languages degree from one of the recently constructed plate glass universities and I'd completed my teaching qualification.

I WAS very keen, enthusiastic, motivated and I'd successfully completed my teaching practice.

Others assured me that teaching was a good job. It was safe and a well-respected career with excellent prospects.

I had three interviews on that day and had the luxury of choice so it seemed an odd and inappropriate question to ask, I naively thought. Not so.

Whilst a number of the stories are about facing a world of hardship, adversity and lack of opportunity, there were many hardworking and delightful pupils who were a credit to the school and their parents, who defied such obstacles and went on to become valuable and respected members of society. It is even more to their credit that they worked alongside some of the larger-than-life, disruptive characters and achieved what they did.

At times for the staff, if you let it, the grind could become soul destroying. We got some things wrong but worked hard, played hard, and very slowly I came to realise what made a successful school tick.

Sometimes I stood well back and watched patiently – and with some trepidation – as others, more experienced, dealt with the most difficult of situations and I learned quickly.

Hopefully the poignancy and triumphs are reflected within these pages.

The first two years of my teaching career was a wonderful time in my life that perhaps can only be appreciated in retrospect.

Every day presented a different, testing challenge. I learned to live on my feet and with my wits about me and it was a vibrant, eye-opening, exciting introduction to the profession.

I was born, went to school in and have never taught anywhere else apart from Yorkshire and have always been extremely proud of that grounding.

It stood me in good stead.

1.

Yorkshire Roots

Dear Miss Padgett,

It all kicked off at our place last night and I am really sorry to have to tell you this. But it really did kick off! That crazy woman from next door has never liked us and thinks she is so much better than us. She is such a silly cow. Any road she only goes and gets her great gorilla of a son to chuck a great big brick through our front room window, doesn't she. Turns out that she's trying to warn us that she don't like our Barry (that's our Jason's big brother, by the way) agreeing to take on some extra work when the unions are dead set against it and her hubby is a big noise in the unions.

It's alright for 'er. Her old man has plenty brass (don't ask no questions) and she 'as at least three cleaning jobs in pubs and clubs (she used to go out with the landlord at the Mucky Ferret, am dead sure) as well as all that money she won down the Bingo and I bet owt that they don't pay all the tax that they should. But that's another story. We really need that job that our Barry got. He's a good worker and he's not interested in all that union rubbish. Never 'as been and never will be! Any road, homework was the last thing on anybody's mind so our Jason didn't do it and that's why I am writing to you so you won't give him any hassle. He has had enough of that to last a lifetime, poor little bugger. She won't get away with it, silly cow.

Thanking you.
Sylvia Dobson

I HAD three interviews for teaching posts on the same day in 1971. If I'm totally honest, I don't recall the criteria I used to help me to decide which particular one to attend, and those to politely and graciously decline. Perhaps my decision was based on geographical location.

I suspect I chose the one which was in the same group I'd completed my second teaching practice in. These groups were called 'pyramids' and they held regular meetings which provided a forum where teachers could exchange ideas on good practice, so easing the transition of pupils from junior to senior school at a crucial time in their young lives.

The one I eventually selected was also the best establishment for me to reach by public transport because I had managed to fail two driving tests in the preceding months.

That I had secured a trio of interviews on the same day was certainly not because I was academically brilliant, far from it.

It was the norm in those days in the late 1960s and early seventies. Teaching was considered to be an excellent career with very good prospects.

New schools and educational initiatives ensured that teachers were in demand and, if I am honest, it never occurred to me in my wildest dreams that I would be unemployed.

Or so I thought. We had been brought up on a diet of government declarations which had assured us that rejuvenated schools were the bright new future and that we were the lucky people who had a huge part to play in this exciting venture.

I gained my first degree, in French, a year previously at a Midlands University and had subsequently come back up North to get married only a month later and was due to embark upon my Post Graduate Certificate in Education course in September 1970.

This, I was led to believe, was when you really got down to the serious business of learning how to teach the practicalities as opposed to all the theoretical and academic assignments.

My chosen course was French with Special Games. I never really understood why they were considered to be special but the title caused me a plenty of embarrassment when subjected to lots of teasing about the possible interpretation.

They were, though, something I enjoyed enormously and provided a welcome break from all the academic and classroom-based work.

I improved my hockey, which I had been playing regularly since I was eleven-years-old and I was also introduced to netball which I had never played at all.

I enjoyed athletics at the university's extensive playing fields and helped to plan and coordinate Sports Days at local schools in preparation for the real thing.

The recently built Sports Hall provided us all with an impressive backdrop where we could practise our indoor sports; my success in this arena was very limited however.

"Are You Strong, Lass?"

I shall never forget the faces of my fellow students and my tutor as I struggled repeatedly in my attempts to get a shuttlecock to make contact with a badminton racket.

The PGCE course required me to attend the local university for approximately two terms and to be attached to local schools for the rest of the time.

Of the many and varied pearls of wisdom which were dispensed during that year, one made a particular impact on my impressionable self. Indeed, it stayed with me right to the very end of my career.

I remember very clearly my tutor Mr Bridges assuring us that he was deadly serious, as he instructed a sceptical audience: "Whenever you are asking a class to do anything, always repeat your instruction at least three times; you must always assume that one third of the class is asleep at any given time."

He actually repeated it three times himself but the humour of it was lost on us.

My first teaching practice placement, at the beginning of the academic year in September 1970, was in an inner city junior school with about 200 pupils who ranged in age from seven to eleven.

I was very excited about my first day in a real school and set off confidently on the two mile walk. I was so proud of my carefully selected outfit – a mini skirt, floral blouse and tank top, shiny, white PVC knee length boots that I paid 49/11d for at Dolcis and an even shinier, bright red PVC raincoat.

I didn't really think that the very fashionable hot pants I'd worn for the preceding few weeks would be inappropriate but my father left me in no doubt about his opinion on the matter as I left.

The school was in a socially deprived area but was a

vital experience for me and, although I was only there for three weeks, I learned numerous valuable lessons, the most useful in humility and the hard facts of life.

The teachers were wonderfully patient, professional people who gave their life to the place and whose modesty was always in evidence.

They were not always appreciated by the parents and often had to battle against seemingly invincible odds in order to make that vital difference to lots of pupils' lives.

They were led by a competent and involved headmaster who was respected by the pupils and teachers alike. He was of the old school then and had his own way of doing things but because he had a seemingly magic ingredient of common sense, his ways were appreciated with excellent results.

The teachers respected their leader because he valued what they did and, in the words of a dear friend of mine in the teaching profession, everyone, "rubbed along very well together."

They welcomed me into their world and shared their knowledge and experience readily and willingly with a very naive and apprehensive young graduate.

Two of the most eye-opening incidents of my entire career occurred in that short period of time as the trees began to change colour to mark the new decade.

The first took place during a music lesson with a class of eight-year-old boys and girls.

Teaching practice students were required to adapt across a wide range of subjects and we were discussing the beat and rhythm of a piece of music.

I was attempting to get the pupils to clap out the beat of the tune and after quite a few practices and demonstrations comparing different walks and movements to the pace of the music, I was confident that they had finally grasped the fundamental principle.

I invited one particularly mischievous-looking little rogue to show us all that he had mastered it.

He was really pleased to be picked and proceeded to clap out the rhythm in his own inimitable fashion, which unfortunately was a million miles away from what we had just practised.

Not wanting to discourage him and also being less than confident in my own ability, I asked him in a low voice if he thought that he had got that quite right.

"Steven, it was supposed to sound like your grandpa walking across the room, wasn't it? Do you remember? Your clapping out of the beat sounded more like somebody clomping around the room with a wooden leg, didn't it?" I questioned.

He looked straight at me with his piercing blue eyes and his lips began to quiver a little. I thought that he was going to burst into tears any minute.

Instead, he managed to find his voice, replying "Well, any road that's how my grandpa walks all t' time because 'e does have a wooden leg."

I just wanted the ground to swallow me up and wondered what the odds were on that happening, I checked it out later and his story was correct.

It must have only been a week or so later when I was flabbergasted once again.

I was with a different class this time, talking about their bedrooms and how a basic plan could be drawn out to scale in their exercise books.

We were discussing the layout of the room, the furniture, the floor covering and what they liked to keep in their room.

I drew a plan on the blackboard and the pupils suggested what went where and why they liked or disliked their room.

I asked them what they kept in their wardrobe and after all the usual answers, one lad was desperate to attract my attention, waving his arms wildly in the air.

"Miss, Miss, there's not none of them sort of things in my cupboard and I bet yer a tanner you'll never guess what is," he assured me.

Paul took a sharp intake of breath, sat up straight in his seat and confidently began his list.

"You'll never guess, Miss, you won't, honest, but here goes! There's a box of watches, loads of Woodbines and other cigs, some posh cufflinks, three transistor radios, thousands and thousands o' Green Shield stamps, some bicycle lamps, some fancy jewellery stuff and a load o' lead that mi old man and our Jez brought home when they stripped that church roof on t'other side o' town last week."

He spoke in a very matter of fact way, not trying to show off or impress anyone.

If he did detect a hint of surprise on my part, or the class's somewhat puzzled expression on the other, then he certainly did not show it.

My subsequent teaching practice placement a term later, after I had supposedly gained more valuable knowledge from attending lectures at university, was in an inner city secondary comprehensive for pupils aged eleven to eighteen. Unlike some other schools in the area it did possess a sixth form.

Once again I encountered many industrious and supremely dedicated teachers who achieved amazing things within the wide spectrum of ability and privilege which existed there.

I did not, however, feel that the leadership was in any way comparable with what I'd previously come across and the results were clear to see in some areas. However, I was very fortunate to receive more valuable advice and guiding principles from my immediate mentors who were always on hand to rescue me from some challenging situations.

The head of modern languages, a chap approaching his retirement, was kindness itself. He could very easily have opted out as he only had a term to go but he remained professional to the end and really went the extra mile for me.

He helped me to prepare for the visits of the external assessor from the university whose job it was to observe me teaching a lesson and grade me accordingly.

Those occasions could be quite intimidating with a class of disaffected fourteen-year-olds but his quiet and unruffled attitude enabled me to sort out and prioritise the things that really mattered in the classroom.

And his many years of dealing with both recalcitrant and gifted children provided me practical coping strategies for the rest of my career.

AS if teaching a foreign language to a group of adolescents was not enough of a challenge, let alone to a trainee teacher, another terrifying ingredient was thrown into the mix - language laboratories.

They were the latest and fashionable facilities to invade schools at the time and deemed to be the answer to a perceived flagging interest in the learning of languages.

Conceptually the concept held strong; pupils could listen to French people speaking real French, could follow and participate in the conversation and, most importantly perhaps, could do it at their own pace within the confines of their own individual headsets.

In theory it sounded wonderful; in practice, it was often very different.

There could be up to twenty-four booths in the laboratory and at the front of the room, the teacher's desk and console were to be found with all the malevolent wires, switches and buttons.

The master tape machine was situated here and enabled the teacher to plug in and communicate on an individual basis with her charges and supposedly monitor progress.

It all terrified me and the more it made me flustered, the more it empowered the pupils. They could obviously smell my fear and sensing that there was sport to be had the boys, in particular, lost no time in taking full advantage of the situation and they transported themselves to an airport control tower.

"This is Daz to Ian. This is Daz to Ian. Can you hear me? I am making an urgent appeal for help right now!" I'd hear. Or, "Coming in to land! Coming in to land! Fuel level is dropping fast! Clear the runway! Roger, over and out!"

The girls were no angels by any means but their foray into the world of technology tended to be on a more basic level where they shrieked and screamed into the microphone about recent developments in their love life.

So I have to confess that, in my lessons at least, the head phones and tapes did not have the desired effect and mastering French was the last thing on most pupils' minds.

Little notice was taken of Miss as she tried in vain to interrupt their conversations and remind them of the real purpose of this fantastic new educational advance.

As if that was not enough to contend with, the operation of the machines was an absolute nightmare for someone technically challenged.

"Are You Strong, Lass?"

The plugs would stick, the wires become tangled and on numerous occasions the whole thing would just grind to a halt, allowing the class to disconnect (both literally and metaphorically) and cause even more mayhem and chaos.

Most of my lessons outside the language laboratory went reasonably well and passed off without any noticeable disaster but not so when being assessed in a games lesson.

It was swimming with a group of about twenty thirteen-year-old girls and was held at the school's own pool which was small but adequate.

All was going well as I had prepared the lesson thoroughly and I knew the group well; my university tutor was seated on a stool, clipboard in hand, ready to note down the highs and the lows of my performance.

ONE of the teachers, Mrs Wall, a thin, wiry lady with a red face who would never see forty again, was keeping a general eye on things as I explained to the girls what I wanted them to do.

For some reason which will remain a mystery until the day I die, Mrs Wall suddenly appeared to turn round on herself, took a couple of steps backwards and promptly fell into the pool.

The sound of a huge splash echoed around the room only to be nearly outdone by the semi-stifled giggles of the girls whose faces were contorted into grotesque patterns.

I cast a quick eye at my tutor who miraculously had managed to keep a straight face and was willing me to do the same.

Somehow, I managed to paint a fixed neutral expression on my rapidly reddening face and to gesture to the girls to assist Mrs Wall out of the pool.

In retrospect, she handled the situation very well

because she just shook herself, gratefully accepted the towel proffered by a bemused pupil and made her way to the changing rooms with an air of remaining dignity which invited all present to conclude that it was something she did every day of her life.

It was never officially mentioned again but I suspect it provided many moments of unadulterated mirth among the girls and among the staff when Mrs Wall was not around.

Talk about being thrown in at the deep end.

I'd endured a rollercoaster term which had been both demanding and rewarding but I very nearly changed my mind about a career in teaching and actually got as far as looking into careers in personnel and hospital almoner positions.

But deep-down my passion was for teaching and I passed my teaching practice and PGCE course and my very first reference from the awarding university was encouraging.

'Mrs Padgett entered this department last October; she had graduated at Warwick in 1970 with a Class 2 Honours in French. She was awarded the Graduate Certificate in Education (with Special Games) in Division 2 in July of this year (1971).

Mrs Padgett is a person with a good sense of humour, which makes her occasional blunt manner acceptable. She made a significant contribution to the work of her tutorial group and enjoyed the discussions in particular. She holds very strong views about education but at least listens to the viewpoints of others.

On teaching practice her performance was competent. She was a hard working and energetic young lady and she showed a keen enthusiasm for her subject. She consistently produced her own teaching materials throughout the period of practice. She had firm control of her classes but at the same time was sensitive to the

23

reactions of her pupils. She was willing to learn and showed
considerable improvement during the term.

We have no hesitation in recommending Mrs Padgett. Her
friendliness and ability as a teacher should make her an asset to a
school staff.

Signed:
L F Bridges, Course Tutor

I WAS not actually in possession of this document on the day
I was due to attend my very first interview.

It was issued a couple of months later and I don't recall
ever showing it to anybody in my entire teaching career.

It was a long walk for that interview, possibly three
miles or so but it seemed more like ten to me.

The white high heeled shoes which I had so confidently
selected from the back of the wardrobe only a couple of hours
earlier, dug into my feet and stabbed me with increasing
ferocity and the muddy grass verges and pebbles underfoot
did nothing to improve the situation.

Vanity does not always pay but those white shoes were
the 'bees' knees,' purchased in the sale at Freeman, Hardy
and Willis.

More importantly, to a twenty-something young lady,
they went perfectly with the bright orange mini dress that I
had just purchased from Etam and which 'fitted where it
touched' as people used to say back then.

I thought it was a stunning combination and just right
to impress.

The school had been designed and constructed only
three or four years previously and was much smaller than the
one where I had done my practice.

It was very different from the Grammar School in Otley
where I had spent my formative years, which had been an

imposing yet very attractive stone-built establishment with a tradition that stretched back centuries.

Was it really only four years since I was a pupil there and had left its safe and protective environment?

I tottered slowly and purposefully down the drive; it was a beautiful sunny day in May and I reached the school's front door.

Stanley Cowburn, the headmaster, was an avuncular sort of chap and he welcomed me warmly into his small and very sparsely furnished office, which was situated right at the front of the building.

In the adjacent office, which was also very small and utilitarian, the school secretary, Pauline Fisher, sat at her desk and peered inquisitively over the top of her typewriter, giving me the once over.

I was to discover subsequently that Mrs Fisher was a big player and what she did not know about the school was really not worth knowing.

Nobody, however important or high up in the educational hierarchy, got past her. She was also a fount of knowledge and a very valuable and loyal member of the staff who was well respected and much loved.

She was always immaculately dressed and took a great pride in her appearance and helped me a lot in that first year and was always on hand to listen when things became just too confusing.

The headmaster quizzed me. Why did I want to teach? What did I see as my strengths? Why had I chosen this school? What did I have to offer?

What I didn't know at the time was that modern languages teachers were a rare commodity, especially in a tough Northern city, and that this school had been without a permanent French teacher for the last two terms.

"Are You Strong, Lass?"

I tried to be honest in my answers and hoped that my genuine desire to get a job would shine through. Deep down I had a good feeling about the place and I was absolutely delighted to be offered the post there and then.

I was the only candidate and so did not have to wait for a week or two for a letter or meet any of the governors and I don't even remember signing a contract or answering any questions about my medical history.

I do remember feeling a warm glow and a secret pride in what I had just achieved.

The icing on the cake was when I was asked by the headmaster if I could start the very next month in June rather than in September.

Could I? A salary, real money and not a student grant – it didn't take long to give him an answer.

I walked out of his office feeling ten feet tall, Mrs Fisher smiled at me as I passed her desk and I was then invited into the staffroom to have a cup of tea and a Players cigarette which I nervously declined, and to complete a very small amount of paperwork with the senior master.

The vast majority of the other staff just carried on with their normal everyday business, some of them didn't even lift their eyes above a copy of the *Yorkshire Post*, through the thick tobacco smoke which hung heavily around the top of their newspaper.

As I left, it was approaching the end of the dinner hour and a number of boys and girls were hanging around the main entrance.

They looked quite a tough bunch but they were on their best behaviour because the senior master was present.

I overheard one of the boys mumble to his mate, "Blimey, Fozzy, I reckon that bird over there is a new teacher!"

Quick as a flash, a rather tarty looking girl with long blond hair who was proudly sporting round, pink national health glasses patched up with pink sticking plaster, shrieked at the top of her voice, "Do ya fancy 'er then, Suggy? Tell 'us, come on!"

I was secretly flattered by the somewhat indiscreet compliment, and thinking that "bird" sounded quite trendy, more so when one of them shouted after me as I disappeared out of the gate, "Bye, then, Miss, we'll see yer next term. If we 'aven't all put yer off and you decide not to come back, that is."

I felt myself blushing as I scuttled away. Miss, he had actually called me miss.

This was it, then, I was going to be a real teacher.

I cast a glance down the drive at the white, modern building which would be my workplace.

The reflections and light patterns created by the strong May sunshine seemed to give the school an almost ghostly and surreal air.

I decided there and then that I would try to rise to the challenge and repay the faith the headmaster had shown in me.

I'd not seen an awful lot of the place or met the bulk of the staff but I did feel that the priorities were right and that they would do their utmost to give these inner city estate kids the best opportunity to succeed.

I was going to try and make a difference and influence children's lives, I couldn't wait to share my good news with my husband and I knew that my Mum and Dad would be so proud of me. I was ready for anything.

2.

Yorkshire Terriers

Dear Miss Padgett,

Me and her dad are not having it. Our Lesley says you made her take her duffle coat off on in the French lesson again yesterday. She feels the cold really badly, you know, and is always getting the sniffles and a bad chest.

How does it all affect learning? What does it matter if her coat is on or off? We kept ours on when we were at school and it didn't do us any harm at all. And I bet those classrooms are just as cold as when I was at school twenty-five years ago.

We have paid a lot of money for that coat (even if we did get it in the C&A sale) and we want her to get all the benefit she can from it. So if you don't mind, please leave her alone and we'll say no more about it.

Yours,
Mrs Janet Roberts

MY first real teaching post turned out to be something of a baptism of fire. I had been at the school for only about a couple of weeks and most of the staff had been very helpful and positive.

"Will you please accompany the J3 boys to the swimming baths?" The words boomed, hollering from the mouth of the Senior Master.

At first I thought it was a great way to start a new career and was quite excited at the prospect. I enjoyed swimming very much and had spent many happy hours as a teenager at my local outdoor baths in Otley, in all seasons and temperatures.

One year I actually managed to get my hands on the much coveted number one season ticket after queuing for hours.

I suppose that I had never really thought about how threatening a group of adolescent boys could be if they put their mind to it.

I'd come across teenagers in my teaching practice and being able to deal with them relatively successfully had involved a lot of hard work and patience, not to mention guts and guile.

But there had usually been someone on hand to help or, in the worst case scenario, bail me out when necessary.

Despite appealing to their better nature, mob rule predominated, testosterone spilled everywhere, and showing off, locking horns and the desire to be the loudest lout took over – it became seriously unpleasant.

It was very new and frightening, and became an extremely delicate situation when I asked or even pleaded with a boy not to do something and he merely replied: "And what you going to do about it, then?"

Ignoring my requests, some of the lads continued to spit out of the bus window and direct their sexist and often obscene comments and inappropriate, well-practised gestures at any female they spied through the window.

The back seat of the bus was a definite no-go area. The lads lolled around, spreading themselves over two seats and some dived dangerously from one to another to the obvious delight of their mates.

As the bus spluttered tentatively into the baths' car park, the twenty lads began to swarm down the aisle enthusiastically pushing, shoving, jeering and hooting at the top of their voices.

Once freed from its constraints, they stampeded into the changing rooms, whooping and yelling for all they were worth, grabbing the metal baskets in which they were theoretically supposed to deposit their clothes.

Towels and kit were strewn everywhere, Spangles papers and distinctive blue, pink and yellow Bazooka Joe bubble gum wrappers and other detritus just abandoned.

The swimming club coach somehow managed to attract their attention and actually teach them. For a short time, as I looked on in amazement and admiration, they actually listened and were anxious to do their best.

It was evident that they wanted to learn all that they could and there were some very talented swimmers in the group.

The coach arranged them in ability groups and set targets and tasks which stretched them all in an appropriate manner for their level and managed to get the best out of the majority of them.

He had earned their respect and had high expectations of them, they wanted to do their best for him and not to let him down.

I discovered later that the school had an enviable reputation for swimming and was the proud winner of many galas and trophies.

Several members of the teaching staff enjoyed swimming and the chemistry teacher, in particular, encouraged the pupils by running after-school coaching sessions.

Many of the children spent a lot of time at the baths in their free time and it was both a useful and worthwhile recreational activity of which their parents approved.

The piercing shrill of a whistle shattering the silence and my temporary reverie, brought me abruptly back to reality, the end of the lesson was nigh and as soon as the coach disappeared, it started all over again.

They were mooning out of the changing cubicles and flicking each other with very rough cotton towels which were even more lethal when wet and which could produce a yelp of pain if applied in exactly the right place on the victim's anatomy.

The noise was unbelievable and almost deafening. I did try to restore order and quell their youthful exuberance and high spirits but nobody was listening.

After what seemed like a dark and threatening eternity, I somehow managed to evacuate the changing rooms and pour them all back on the bus much to the barely disguised amusement of the coach, who had undoubtedly seen it all before.

It was only a five minute ride back to school but seemed like a two hour expedition.

"Thanks, Miss! That were right good o' yer to tek us, seein' 'ow Dusty Miller were poorly this week. ''Appen we'll see yer again next week! What's yer name, by the way?" squeaked one of the more mild–mannered as several of the harder elements glared at both him and me with scornful disdain.

I was shell-shocked but, as time went on, I did succeed in asserting my authority gradually and setting a good example whenever and wherever I could.

I think that it would be fair to say that I eventually gained the respect of most of my pupils – even J3 – but it was something I had to work very hard at and it was not given away lightly or carelessly.

Any relationships with young people, especially those who had much to contend with in their lives, had to be built on trust.

If nobody had shown them much love, care or respect, then it was always going to be difficult for them in turn, to display any back.

It was not always appropriate or desirable to discipline them harshly but neither was it right to be too lenient; the balance was crucial and perhaps gave real meaning to the phrase 'tough love.' It was a combination which often saved them from themselves.

Many of those unruly boys eventually turned out to be good citizens and family men. At least three of them signed as professional rugby league players for local clubs, a couple became musicians and at least one secured a part in a well-known film. Several of them lived and worked in the area for many years and their children eventually became pupils at the school.

Regrettably, but perhaps predictably, a small number of them were detained at Her Majesty's Pleasure for quite some time and continued to be a constant source of irritation to all around them for the rest of their lives.

They had practised and perfected that particular skill at school.

Fridays were always different and seemed to have a life of their own. 'Happy Fridays' they were affectionately known as among the teaching staff or occasionally we referred to them as 'poets' day' (piss off early tomorrow's Saturday)

It was undoubtedly the kids' favourite day of the week too and the only one when the evil smell of boiled fish escaped from the school kitchen and infiltrated the entire school.

Friday finishes were always welcome, especially after a long session with K4 Girls. There were not many of them and they were an academically challenged group but what they lacked in numbers, they certainly made up for with evil.

Kim, Sandra and Alison were hard work at the best of times but on a Friday they really came into their own.

Whatever strategy I employed or desperate measures I took, nothing could persuade them to pay attention and attempt to learn something meaningful or even to listen.

They were just not interested and couldn't be bothered. It was Friday, the beginning of the weekend and that meant one thing to them, freedom!

They could meet their boyfriends and do numerous unmentionable things, although I soon found out that they were more than happy to describe exactly what they intended to do to any poor unsuspecting person around who was in earshot.

They had the chance to escape from their parents and head off into town to buy their Rimmel make up, perfumes from Woolworths, records and unsuitable magazines and, best of all, they did not have to go to school for two whole glorious days.

It was a difficult and demanding situation and twenty minutes at least of every lesson was spent trying to persuade them to remove their coats.

"Are You Strong, Lass?"

Whatever the weather, there was no way that they were going to be parted from them. The khaki-coloured parka and its threatening furry hood seemed to be a badge of honour. It almost had a life of its own and it was a huge status symbol.

It was not even part of the official school uniform but that seemed of little importance to them at the time.

The sun could be beating down fiercely and the temperature steadily rising but still they clung on to their beloved parkas as if they were a second skin or even an alter ego.

Sandra North was one of the more challenging culprits. She would sit malevolently, hunched up at the back of the classroom with her arms tightly wrapped around her and visibly and silently dare anyone to challenge her about her beloved garment.

Long and many were the arguments I had with her, trying to assert my authority and make her see reason.

But I couldn't, I did not at that time have either the strategies or the guile to outwit her.

If those pupils had only known the feelings of fear and trepidation I felt as a newly qualified teacher walking through that classroom door, the situation would have been even more disastrous.

Every Friday dinner time, without fail, one or two teachers could be spotted lurking and shuffling awkwardly near the register racks just outside the office, pleading with the Education Welfare Officer and imploring her not to go and seek out those children who were represented by blood-red noughts in the morning register.

The prospect of some of those noughts transforming themselves into afternoon attendances was more than most could contemplate.

Surely, instead, there was some paperwork that she

could catch up on instead of searching the estate looking for the absent miscreants and bringing them back into school; it would hardly make the slightest difference to their education.

Quite often the pleading worked and peace prevailed.

Other devious and rather Machiavellian schemes were employed as and when the need arose and whenever nerves were frayed and tolerance exhausted.

I found myself one fateful Friday afternoon having to cover a lesson for an absent colleague with a Lower Band group of boys in Year Three, aged thirteen and fourteen.

I hadn't actually taught them before but their reputation preceded them so I was under no illusion as to what I was up against.

My colleague had left a well-prepared lesson for them but they did not want to know and were just not in the mood.

In addition, it was a very windy afternoon with a gale howling outside the classroom windows, a meteorological phenomenon which never failed to turn a well-behaved class into a noisy bunch. No amount of cajoling, threatening or bribing could distract these lads from their indolence and apathy.

I tried a trick I'd gleaned from a more mature colleague who had seen it all.

He worked on the assumption that a lot of bad behaviour was down to a child's perception of what he could or could not do; it therefore followed that if that child was given a task that was tangible and which resulted in some sort of achievement, then there was some small chance of compliance and possibly the opportunity to engage the pupil more positively at some time in the future.

So, on a wild and windy Friday afternoon, on the top corridor of an inner city secondary school, that plan was unleashed as a last desperate measure.

"Are You Strong, Lass?"

It was quite simply a pile of *Autocar* and *Car* magazines strategically placed at the back of the classroom on the floor in a complete mess, which needed putting in chronological date order.

The task kept the hard core of troublemakers gainfully employed for the whole lesson and allowed some of the quieter lads to actually do some work.

It sounds ridiculous and defeatist but it worked. To them, it was a structured task with a beginning, a middle and an end, but, more importantly, a purpose.

Once the mission was accomplished some of them would even settle down and actually try to read the magazines and look at the photographs.

The icing on the cake was that it could all be set up again immediately in time for the next lesson.

The space between the lessons was more than adequate to set the trap once again as this type of class was thankfully rarely, if ever, on time.

One quick and meaningful push and all the magazines were all over the floor in disarray once more.

That first lesson on a Monday morning was also always interesting for a wide variety of colourful reasons.

Admittedly, much depended on which particular class was destined to beat its reluctant way to your door but if it was an underwhelmed group of fifteen year olds, you just knew you were in for a challenging ride.

The first task, whatever the prevailing circumstances, was to ascertain that the class realised that it was Monday morning and that it was back in school; the weekend was over and the menu was different.

As this message was being delivered, there was much yawning, shuffling, farting and whispering as a sea of blank and uninterested faces met my gaze.

On the one hand, some of the kids had endured a hard and demanding weekend through no fault of their own, many had needed to take on jobs which by rights were nothing to do with them.

They had been required to feed and care for younger siblings, do the shopping, clean the house and adopt the role of general dogsbody.

And despite that, it would have been a good weekend if they had not been exposed to any sort of abuse, whether it was verbal, sexual, physical or emotional.

It perhaps took me far too long to conclude that the last thing we should have pestered these poor unfortunates with the first thing on a Monday morning, was whether they had completed their homework or if they had a sharp pencil or a pen.

They had had much more pressing and urgent situations with which to deal and so many of them were mentally and physically inadequately equipped to attempt to do so.

It was to their great credit that they even turned up at school at all but, then again, they knew what to expect there and that, at least, they were safe – not that they would have ever dreamt of admitting it.

The fortunate ones in the group had possessed the dubious privilege of being masters of their own destiny instead.

They had enjoyed two whole days where they had been lucky enough to please themselves, well away from the interfering and prying eyes of parents and teachers alike.

Monday morning came as a dreadful shock to the system as they tried in vain to adjust to a more structured and boring routine.

Bleary eyed and ashen faced, the boys in particular

would struggle to convince anyone that they were actually present in the same universe as anyone else, let alone the same classroom.

Occasionally, they would appear to burst into some sort of life and would alternate between delivering graphic, lurid accounts of what they had got up to over the weekend and dramatically proving the point from time to time by throwing up all over the desk in front.

Looking back I wonder how we actually did all survive but we did.

Lots of things were called into play including humour, patience, grit, awkwardness and skill, but above all perhaps was the solidarity and friendship which existed between the members of staff.

On some occasions the almost black humour of the situation would overwhelm us all and things were rendered totally futile and seemingly pointless as we collapsed in fits of hysterical laughter in the relative safety of the staffroom.

And the pupils did appreciate it all in their own way. They seemed to possess a rather weird sense of loyalty which was somewhat unexpected but very moving.

They would defend you to the hilt if they thought you deserved it and served your time.

I fondly recall one time involving a new boy called Keith Duckett who had recently moved into the area from a school in London.

He was a nice enough lad with a very strong cockney accent but admittedly he was rather a show off and he liked the sound of his own voice far too much which was a dangerous trait in our part of the world.

His surname was made for rhyming couplets and settling the class down in an attempt to complete any work was a regular and ongoing battle.

Keith had taken exception to something and was trying to clarify a point of grammar. He wasn't actually arguing with me but his voice was raised and he was gesticulating wildly.

The boys in the class seized the opportunity to have some sport at his expense and to demonstrate that they could be quite protective of me when it suited them.

Of course, they were not the least bit interested in the mysteries and complexities of French infinitives but they could not afford to lose face.

Kenneth Lloyd, who was perhaps one of the biggest rogues in the year group, appointed himself as class spokesman and proudly delivered his speech in front of the enthralled group.

"Don't you worry, miss," he began. "We'll look after you, we'll sort it out. Coming up here from snobby down South and bringing all 'is posh ways with 'im, who does 'e think 'e is?

"Shurrup, Keith and sit down right now before we mek yer and stop talking rubbish. Leave 'er alone, she's all right. She don't deserve to be spoken to in that way, does she?

"If anybody's going to rattle 'er cage, it's us and not you. You can't talk to 'er like that but we can, so back off sharpish or we'll shove yer 'ead down 'bog at break!"

It was the best sort of back-handed compliment.

Nobody had ever talked to poor Keith like that before and his face was a picture. He backed off, scurried back to his chair and buried his head in his text book, taking no more part in that particular lesson.

He had just been given a lesson in Northern loyalty and plain speaking.

As time went on, he was eventually accepted by the gang after he had successfully passed more initiation tests.

"Are You Strong, Lass?"

Dear Miss,

I am writing to you to ask if you can please arrange for someone to move our Kevin in his maths lessons. He just seems to get into loads of trouble sitting next to that Peter Smales. They never got on with each other when they were at the juniors either and I did ask that they were put in separate classes but for some reason, it didn't happen.

I know well enough that our Kevin is no angel but he says that Peter keeps kicking him in the balls and shoving a ruler down his trousers so he can't concentrate on his work. If you could please move him without him knowing that I have been in touch because he would kill me! Much appreciated.

Thanks a lot.
Maureen Riley

3.

Yorkshire Dialect

Dear Miss,

I am really sorry to have to tell you this, but here goes!

That right expensive new French text book you sent home with our Barry and that hadn't to be lost or damaged on any account, well it has been. Lost that is.

We've looked all over the house. Well, I have, but Barry's dad just don't go in for that sort of thing, women's work, he says. I have looked in all the usual places like under beds, in the kitchen, down the back of the big armchair and even in the shed at the allotment. We found a whole load of stuff that's been missing for ages and some Playboy *magazines but no luck with that French book, though.*

We will have another good search and am going to pluck up the courage to finally get round to bottoming our Barry's bedroom properly. But, I really do have to get mi' head straight before I can face it all.

"Are You Strong, Lass?"

Don't crack on to our Barry, though, because he'll likely go bananas. I will keep you posted and am really sorry again. Hoping you will be understanding in this matter. I suppose that you better let me know if I owe you any money. Hope not because brass is tight enough as it is.

Yours,
Sylvia Andrews

I HAD completed my degree in French only one year previously and as I entered my first classroom in my new school, I felt a huge feeling of trepidation.

What if nobody listened? What if they all laughed at me? What if nobody was the least bit interested in what I had to say?

I had completed a reasonably successful teaching practice at a similar establishment but this was very different.

The year was 1971 and the teaching of modern languages was very much at the forefront of educational thinking. Recent local and national schemes had seen much emphasis placed on the introduction of a foreign language at a young age and it was seen as vital to ensure that all the good practice established at junior level continued at secondary school.

Meetings were set up to ensure a smooth transition in order to provide the optimum chances and opportunities for the children.

Numerous courses abounded and there was a mountain of literature to read and inwardly digest.

I was extremely fortunate that the lady in charge of French at the local junior school was wonderful and talented and she gave me so much support and help in those early days.

Irene and I met regularly, talked about the new initiatives and discussed the pupils who would eventually transfer from her school to mine.

She was so dedicated and professional as well as very approachable and she made a huge impression on me.

I'd like to think that some of my eventual success in teaching was partly down to the example that she set for me and the sheer enthusiasm and love she displayed towards her subject.

The pupils loved her because she cared about them and wanted them to do well, she became a lifelong friend and I enjoyed many happy social events with her and her family before her cruel and untimely death.

Looking back many years later, it struck me just how important my contact with this very special lady had been.

She was full of common sense and did not believe in jumping on every bandwagon that happened to come along.

At the same time she was very receptive to new ideas once she'd had the necessary time to assess them properly.

She possessed huge amounts of empathy and was always on hand to offer me sound advice which stood me in good stead for many years to come.

Her support and guidance was particularly important because I found it hard to relate to some of the ideas espoused by some members of the local authority advisory service.

I was extremely confused and puzzled after a visit from the French advisor who had come to observe me in my first term of teaching.

I was told in no uncertain terms that I was not to write any French spellings on the blackboard because it would upset and confuse the pupils and: "It really was not necessary, dear."

I didn't understand his viewpoint at all because I felt

43

that it was a vital part of learning even though techniques and teaching methods were in a state of change then.

I expressed a rather guarded opinion and was talked down and browbeaten with a lot of fancy words and rhetoric and I had to agree to go along with the new ideas or at least pay lip service to them.

When I was on my own in the classroom, with only the kids watching me, I wrote the spellings on the blackboard as often and as defiantly as I could, making firm and bold strokes with the sticks of white chalk.

The children copied them carefully into their little green vocabulary books and took them home to learn by heart for a spelling test.

It stood them in good stead and gave them a firm foundation on which to build their foreign language studies.

I don't think it stifled their creativity or made them feel awkward or disadvantaged and it helped them to build their confidence and train their memories.

The first text book I used was called *En Avant* and was published by Nuffield.

It was a new course and had been devised to promote the different approach to language teaching; audio visual methods were emphasised and a huge move towards conducting the entire lesson in the target language were now accepted as the norm.

It was a far cry from the dull and foreboding volume which I had used at grammar school in the late fifties.

This bright red, colourful tome possessed a wide variety of exercises based on reading, listening, speaking and writing.

Flash cards, films and tape recordings were a vital part of the lessons and the characters of Xavier, Brigitte, Georges and Marie seemed to skip through the pages and invite the pupils along with them to share their adventures, rather than drag them unwillingly as in my day.

Many of the teaching topics featured the Basque area of France near to Spain and followed the adventures of a smuggling gang.

I must admit that I found it a rather odd choice of subject matter and geographical area but it certainly did add a little glamour and excitement to the subject.

I recall with great affection one young lady in Class J5, aged thirteen.

Lisa Roland was as round as she was tall. She loved French with a passion and was always keen and eager to participate as much as she could and whenever she could.

She was in the bottom stream in the year group yet that was not going to stop her.

"Can wi do them colours again Miss? Go on, s'il vous plaît."

So we did, over and over again as I pointed to my chart.

"Le ciel est de quelle couleur?" "C'est bleu, Madame!"

"Et la robe de Brigitte?" "C'est rouge, Madame!"

"Le chien de Paul, il est noir ou blanc?"

"Noir, Madame!"

This would go on week after week and Lisa and many of her classmates just could not get enough.

It was an excellent way to open the lesson and along with other oral exercises formed a firm basis for the very slow and gradual progression into slightly more demanding exercises.

We would act out some of the little dialogue situations and I can picture Lisa to this very day, taking a sharp intake of breath, tossing her head back and declaiming loudly and proudly, "Suivez-moi au poste de Police!"

A lot of those less able kids derived great benefit from

these lessons and although I didn't necessarily always realise it at the time, I gradually became aware of the special buzz they derived.

Nobody would claim there were linguists among them or that they were going to aspire to the academic heights.

But what was more important was the fact that they themselves knew that they were not.

As long as they felt that they had achieved, albeit modestly, within that lesson and among an equal peer group, then it gave them confidence on which to build.

I like to think that it helped them in other areas of the curriculum as well.

I have always been a great believer in unlocking children's confidence and giving them a feeling of self-worth and self-esteem.

The subject is almost irrelevant because they will approach it with some sort of inner belief that they can do it.

French perhaps had an added attraction in that it was a blank sheet on which to write.

It didn't matter that they always found spelling in English very challenging or almost impossible to learn their times tables; French was a whole new world for them where they could start again and learn their numbers and colours a week at a time if necessary.

While they were learning and achieving, they were getting well-deserved recognition and I knew that it felt so good to some of them.

Of course not every child in the group enjoyed the subject or wanted to be involved; for every Lisa there was at least one Duncan Brand.

To say that they did not like each other would be a huge understatement. They lost no opportunity to insult each other or catch each other out.

Whenever Lisa's enthusiasm for her favourite subject got the better of her, she would launch herself across the desk with little if any regard for decorum or modesty, showing her slightly grubby paper nylon underskirt and knickers to everyone in the room.

This would give her arch enemy the chance he needed to humiliate her further. Shouting at the top of his voice, he would shriek out his infamous insult which we all got sick of hearing: "Blimey, look at 'er! Sights yer see when yer 'aven't yer gun!"

No sooner had the words escaped from his lips than Lisa jumped off the desk and grabbed his long greasy hair and stuck her nails into his face, all the while hollering at the top of her voice and questioning his parentage.

His one and only ambition was to disrupt the lesson as quickly and effectively as possible, whilst at the same time attracting an enthralled and adoring audience and he succeeded on several occasions.

Duncan demolished many lessons piece by piece with stupid questions, caustic comments at inappropriate times and wearing with pride the hat of the class clown as often as he could, not least in continually questioning the sexuality of lead character Xavier (which he pronounced it Ex-av - i- her)

His remark would be met by hoots of raucous laughter and jeering from the lads on one side of the classroom but Lisa Roland and her friends bravely ignored him and his partners in crime as much as they could and continued to derive great benefit and recognition from the lessons.

They loved the flip charts and flash cards and absolutely adored the tape recordings, answering eagerly in the pauses after the beeps and squealing with delight when their efforts were acknowledged as correct.

They waited with eager anticipation for the cine films

and slides which showed them pictures of people and places they had never seen before and temporarily luxuriated in their new world and its alluring enticements to escape their mundane existence.

I loved delivering these lessons and watching the pupils' reactions although I must confess to fearing and at time hating the technological challenges that they brought with them.

Screens, projectors and tape recorders which all had to be operated simultaneously fed my nightmares for many years.

Kids would unplug things behind your back, change the tapes, switch the lights on and off at the wrong time and be generally the biggest nuisance they could.

Being a glutton for punishment, I did try to go that extra mile for those lower ability classes.

I encouraged them to bring 'anything French' into school on certain days so that we could create a display or play at shops.

A cornucopia of goodies arrived; pictures of the Eiffel Tower, travel brochures, magazine cuttings of pictures of French cheeses, empty wine bottles – often including Blue Nun and Mateus Rose – and grandpa's medal that he had been awarded in the war for winning: "A big battle in France and killing a lot of them Jerries, Miss!"

We followed the Tour de France in the newspapers and made displays and montages for the classroom walls. We loved reading about the winner of each stage and colouring in his maillot jaune with our yellow pencils.

We played at shops and planned and designed our own posters. We drew and coloured in numerous tricolores and sketched bunches of grapes and baguettes.

I lost count of the times I was asked about French

Letters and whether they were different from English letters. I can still hear the giggles when the words for swimming pool and ski slope were identified.

The words would dance on the lips of several of the lads for the majority of the lesson and they would shout them out at the top of their voice as they all got squashed in the rush escaping from the classroom at the end of the lesson.

"Piste off you!" "And you can Piscine off as well!"

On some occasions, I would find them hunched up on the floor of the playground at break, thumbing through a French dictionary that they had 'borrowed' from the library, looking for the equivalent of the raciest words.

Fortunately, they couldn't spell intercourse in English.

Even the more academically inclined pupils possessed very little in the way of extra help.

Occasionally, someone might come into class clutching a tiny battered French dictionary which had belonged to Mum or a well-thumbed phrase book that had actually been to Paris when Auntie Sheila had undertaken a risqué weekend.

There were always those interesting moments, at the most inappropriate time, when the kids would corner and interrogate you.

They would obtain a French dictionary from the library and search out the most obscure and longest word they could find, pronounce it as well as they could and then demand an immediate and accurate translation.

Any hesitation was seen as weakness, most of the words tended to be of a sexual nature and the inevitable reaction awaited with bated breath.

Nor was the need for instant translation confined to the classroom.

At the end of a stressful day, finally relaxing in the

staffroom with a well-earned cup of tea, so I thought, I received a panic phone call from a friend in the garage business.

One of their customers had broken down in the south of France and was failing miserably in all attempts at communication with a local garage.

I was asked if I could speak to the garage owner there on his behalf and sort out things to everyone's mutual satisfaction.

Crankshaft? Big end? Fan belt? I hardly knew what they were in English let alone in French but muddled through somehow.

I received a beautiful bouquet of flowers for my troubles which was very welcome.

On another occasion, there was a Sirdar factory in the town which exported knitting wool and produced patterns and information sheets and one of the girl's mums worked there.

I found Alison hovering nervously at my desk just before the bell for registration.

"Miss, Miss, you've got to help us. My mum has brought home all these knitting pattern books and her boss has told her that she has to sort them out so that she can get an order ready for somebody really important, and, and, and everything's written in flipping French, with lots of long words," she spat out assertively and very out of character.

Immediately realising her unintended rudeness, she blushed and shuffled about uncomfortably.

I reassured her that I would do my very best for her mum. She left them with me and I managed to make some sort of sense of the encrypted and mysterious codes.

It has to be said that I enjoyed rather limited success and struggled to understand a lot of it.

However, I managed to do enough to please Alison's mum and delight her daughter who from that day forth was of the mind that I could translate absolutely anything into French.

My undeserved reward was a small box of Milk Tray which I was pleased to humbly accept.

Dear Miss,

What time does it start? I suppose I do need to talk to you about our Hilary and her French lessons, even if I am not that keen and can't really spare the time to trail up to school in this lousy weather. Besides I want to watch On the Buses *on the telly*

Thank you.
Mrs L Spalding.
PS. I mean that Parents Evening tomorrow.

4.

Yorkshire Grit

Dear Mrs Padgett,

I regret to inform you that John will not be in school for the rest of the week. As you will have gathered from the recent coverage in newspapers and on the television, there was a dreadful accident at Silvers Dale Pit two days ago. Six miners were killed when an underground seam was flooded. What you may not know, however, is that one of the six men killed was our John's uncle, Michael.

He is obviously devastated along with the rest of the family, especially his mother, Michael's sister Debra, and there are lots of things that we have to attend to. We know that the school will be extremely supportive and I would like to thank you all in advance. He will of course return to school as soon as we all feel it is the right time and we feel that he will cope with this very sad situation.

Yours sincerely,
Philip Brook

I SOON discovered that tragedy was capable of striking at random both inside and outside the classroom.

I had been teaching for only about a year or so when I was witness to such a terrible and tragic event.

It was a very ordinary and dull day in late February. We had just returned to school after the half-term break and it was the end of a routine morning.

I heard the chattering and bustle of the third form girls as they made their way to the changing rooms after their netball lesson.

There was nothing new in that as excited young voices exchanged secrets and shared experiences, all of them glad to be inside once again where they could attempt to warm up their frozen limbs.

I was doing some work alone in the staffroom, catching up on some marking in a rare free period, when suddenly there was a sharp and urgent knocking on the door.

I opened it promptly and was met by one of the girls, standing there awkwardly and looking wide-eyed and eerily pale.

"Miss, Mrs Woodhead says please can somebody go right away to the headmaster's office and tell him that that Mrs Woodhead would like him to come as quickly as possible please to the changing rooms?"

"Yes, of course, Sharon," I replied, trying not to sound too anxious and puzzled at the same time.

I followed her a little way on the corridor and as she made her way across the hall back to the changing rooms.

I tentatively knocked on the headmaster's closed, somewhat forbidding door and awaited a response.

The school secretary was not in school that day and a rather gruff voice shouted, "Yes? What is it? Come in, please."

I relayed the girl's somewhat puzzling message as best I could to the Headmaster and almost immediately he rose from his chair purposefully and strode out of his office.

He nodded his head at me as he set off, indicating that he would deal with it and that I was not to accompany him.

The next time I cast eyes on him was when he was making that same journey back again some ten minutes later.

Gone was the familiar purposeful stride and the air of authority which had been replaced by a heavy and laboured gait and an ashen, disbelieving face.

His eyes were almost expressionless and staring and he seemed to have aged at least ten years. He appeared to shuffle into the relative shelter of his office but he was not in there for long.

After a hastily snatched private moment to take in the enormity of the dreadful situation, he was in the staffroom imparting the chilling news to the teaching staff, who had been called in from all corners, and was attempting to assist us in trying to make some sort of sense of it all.

What had awaited him in those changing rooms was every teacher's nightmare and worst case scenario.

A girl had collapsed shortly after coming in from the netball court. Mrs Woodhead, one of the P E teachers, had assessed the situation quickly and, realising that it was a very serious matter had sent for senior help.

In spite of her prompt response and very professional handling of this dreadful event, by the time the Headmaster had made that short walk across the hall, the girl had died in her arms.

What followed was a mixture of so many different things. Disbelief, shock, anger, panic, tears, and desperate pain were all tightly woven into that dreadful tapestry.

The girl was thirteen years old and apparently in good

health, she'd helped her team to victory by scoring the only goal of the match.

It transpired much later after the subsequent inquest that she had suffered a massive brain haemorrhage.

The Headmaster handled everything so well, balancing efficiency and calm with his own inner feelings of obvious despair.

Practicalities were dealt with promptly and sensitively and the raw reality of the situation hit me very hard indeed.

I was only about ten years older than the girl and had never experienced anything like it before, I knew nothing of death.

A horrible irony was that the girl's parents were funeral directors and the job of breaking the terrible news to them fell to two senior teachers.

Both of them were visibly stunned and shaken when they returned to school later in the day.

The pupils were, understandably, heartbroken, scared and confused.

A special assembly was called to explain the tragic situation to them all and the hall was awash with a sea of puzzled and innocent faces, wondering why Mr Cowburn had needed yet another assembly that day.

They listened in stunned silence to the carefully chosen words of the Headmaster, only gently interrupted occasionally by the quiet sobbing of her classmates.

I shall never forget the foreboding sight of the empty desk at afternoon registration and the tortured faces of her friends who were so vulnerable and so young.

This was long before the days of counselling and public displays of affection, the afternoon lessons continued in as normal a way as they could and the school was not closed even on the day of her funeral.

It was not out of any lack of respect or insensitivity, just the way things were dealt with in that era.

I was very impressed with the way in which it was handled and was soon to come to realise that even when problems abounded on a daily basis they were dealt with promptly, firmly and fairly.

Everyone worked together, there was no passing the buck.

A week or so later the following headline appeared in the local paper, 'Girl dies after game of netball.'

While this was literally true, her death was not as a result of the netball match and the headline caused a lot of anxiety and confusion.

Understandably, many parents panicked and jumped to the wrong conclusion and another lesson I learned was never to believe everything I read in the newspapers.

Indeed, a netball match played only a few weeks after could have caused much unnecessary panic and misunderstanding if it had not been, again, handled promptly and sensitively.

One of the girls was hit hard by the ball full in the face which caused her spectacles to smash and cut her face.

Some of the pupils had seen the blood pouring down her face and had immediately envisaged another grim and grotesque situation playing out in front of them.

Fortunately, once more the members of staff were there for those girls and they were helped to conquer that particular demon.

It was a big thing for me to take on board so early in my career and it undoubtedly left its mark.

Memories were reignited a few years later when the girl's younger sister became a pupil at school.

How hard must it have been for those poor parents to

even walk through the main door once more with all its tragic memories, let alone embrace the school again for another three years to enable their daughter to receive a good education?

But they did, and they regularly thanked the staff for the sensitive way in which their elder daughter's untimely death had been handled at the time.

I was amazed at their courage and guts and never forgot them or their bravery.

As a young teacher, I was surprised initially at how quickly the pupils became part of my extended family; I was also surprised how fond I found myself becoming of so many of them. Sometimes they needed a lot of guidance and reassurance; on other occasions a quick kick up the pants and a dose of tough love.

However, there were those times when they simply needed protecting because they were children, like my intervention in a case of physical violence against a fourteen year old girl.

Aisha was the daughter of a white English-born mother and an Asian father who had come to England in his early teens with his family.

She was a lovely and vibrant girl who was very popular with staff and pupils alike, of average ability but always gave of her best and was keen and motivated.

She had settled into school very well and was very much part of the social scene, joining in with all the out-of-school activities and enjoyed some success on the sports field.

One morning, I noticed that she seemed a little on edge and ill-at-ease in the lesson, which was unusual for Aisha and that was precisely why I picked up on it.

I had a quiet word with her at the end of the lesson but she assured me that all was well and that she was just tired.

"Are You Strong, Lass?"

As she turned to make her way out of the classroom, her hand seemed to move almost involuntarily to the right hand side of her neck, and a very slight intake of breath escaped from her lips.

Her face said it all, she was in a lot of pain and discomfort. Her eyes met mine and I knew that she wanted me to intervene and yet at the same time she wished that she was a million miles away.

I moved closer to her and where her blouse collar had been displaced by her hand, I spotted some redness on her neck.

As soon as she realised what I'd seen, she burst into tears and crumpled into a nearby chair.

I put my arm around her and asked her if she wanted to tell me anything.

She took my hand and placed it on her neck.

On closer examination, I could see several angry-looking marks and deep red abrasions which covered a large part of her neck.

I must have been visibly shocked because the only words the poor lass could manage to utter were, "Sorry Miss."

Much heartache and soul-searching followed, both in the immediate aftermath and in the weeks that followed.

It eventually came to light that her father could not cope with his little girl becoming a young woman and all that went with it.

He was jealous of her friendship groups, both boys and girls, and resented her desire to enjoy western activities which were an everyday part of life for her school friends.

His immediate and very misguided response was to wrap a leather belt tightly around her neck and pull it hard until he got the reaction and compliance he wanted.

Her mother was aware of this cruel act and had played no active part in it but she knew better than to interfere with her husband's decisions on any matter and so chose not to intervene.

The immediate concern was naturally for Aisha's safety and well-being and I, along with other members of staff, met with several support agencies as a matter of some urgency and she was placed with foster parents in a 'safe house.'

I remember taking her to the house in the evening accompanied by a senior colleague and I will never forget the look of gratitude on her young face.

I still pass that house frequently on my way into town and can never look at it without thinking about Aisha.

She settled well and was able to have regular access visits to her mother with whom she had a strong bond.

She eventually went on to attend the local college to complete her education and secured a job in catering which she loved.

I kept in touch with her for several years and we would occasionally meet for a coffee in town.

Another young girl stayed in my thoughts for many years and sadly for very similar and dark reasons.

Yvonne Jefferson slipped under the radar, she had come to us at the age of eleven from the local junior school with a rather depressing but not unusual background history.

There had been meetings between us and the liaison staff and the school was made aware that the family was not at all cooperative in any matters regarding school.

Yvonne's attendance was very patchy, she rarely handed in any homework, was frequently in the wrong uniform or without games kit, on the free school dinner register and, all in all, a disadvantaged figure who did not have a lot going for her at all.

"Are You Strong, Lass?"

She came from a large family and spent a lot of her time looking after the younger ones.

At school she at least got a break from the inappropriate daily grind to which she had sadly become so accustomed.

She didn't excel nor had a huge circle of friends, but she got by, just.

We helped her as much as we could but we were held back because her home situation was not deemed to be chaotic or negative enough for such as Social Services to be brought in.

Yvonne's favourite days were when some sort of sporting activity featured.

During the periods of cold weather, she was certainly not one of the ever increasing group of girls who would do anything to avoid going out to the hockey pitch, producing some lame note from home of varying authenticity as to why they couldn't participate.

She loved most sports and was happy to be outside in the fresh air where she could be herself and free from all the burdens which weighed heavily on her at home.

Yvonne particularly enjoyed P.E., especially the game of 'pirates', played at the end of each term as a treat.

It involved the gymnasium being set out with all the apparatus – boxes, vaulting horses, the buck, benches, rubber mats – which, along with the wall bars and ropes, provided a huge and challenging arena in which to spar.

Two pupils were appointed as the pirates and they had to pursue the others across the obstacles in order to catch them and 'tig' them.

The pirates would wear a coloured band across their gym shirt to identify them and it was a great source of pride to be chosen.

The pupils would leap confidently from one piece of

apparatus to another, perhaps recklessly at times, all the while desperately trying to keep their feet off the ground, which we all pretended was the sea.

A member of staff kept a watchful eye on proceedings, blowing her whistle from time to time to indicate a breach of the rules.

It was after a session of 'pirates' that I was presented with a delicate situation.

The showers, which the pupils were obliged to use after all games lessons, were not only cold but communal.

Apart from a few complaints and the odd mutterings, they were all quite happy to parade through the chilly cascading waters, occasionally stopping and pretending to wash themselves with disgusting looking bars of evil smelling carbolic soap.

Obviously there was no place to hide and most of the girls were anxious to go through as quickly as possible and escape to the relative cover of their towel in the changing rooms in order to hide their developing bodies as quickly as possible.

It was while I was encouraging some of the girls to hurry up and perhaps consider quelling their incessant chatter, that I caught sight of a very large purple mark in the middle of Yvonne's back.

She realised that I had seen it and she tried very hard to avoid making eye contact with me and shuffled back to her peg to get dressed.

As the changing room slowly emptied and the girls made their way to other lessons, I quietly beckoned her to come over to me. She looked awkward and rather sheepish and stared pointedly at her feet.

"Miss, I know what you're going to say, but it's all right. Honest it is," she mumbled.

"And what am I going to say, Yvonne?" I responded quietly, hoping to tease something out of her gently.

"You're gonna go on about that bruise, aren't you? Well, I tripped over our Tommy's scooter last night and landed right awkwardly. It didn't half hurt," she said hurriedly, feeling a little more confident that I might accept this seemingly plausible explanation.

I looked at her and caught her off guard for a split second but it was just long enough to detect some uncertainty in her eyes and general demeanour.

"You do know you can talk to me about anything, don't you, Yvonne? You can trust me if there is something you need to say."

She remained motionless on the spot, head down with her whole body almost frozen.

"Come on Yvonne, love, let me help you. We get on well, don't we?"

Gradually, she lifted her head to reveal red and watery eyes and a look of panic and fear etched on her face.

"I suppose I deserved it, Miss. I had been getting on his nerves when he was trying to listen to them football pool results and earlier when 'e were trying to sort out the Spot the Ball thing in 'is newspaper," she ventured tentatively amid muffled sobs.

After a few more exchanges, it sadly transpired that Yvonne's father had 'brayed' her for being a, "bloody annoying little brat" and what was even sadder was that it was by no means the first time.

She informed me that he just lost his rag and didn't really mean it.

I listened to her as she unburdened herself, describing the numerous other occasions on which she had been subjected to his various unwelcome attentions.

I pointed out gently to her that we could help her and that she did not need to suffer any more abuse.

As soon as that word was mentioned, she clammed up and would not talk to me for a while.

It was almost as if that description catapulted everything into a very different arena and one in which she was no longer prepared to fight.

"I don't want nobody else involved, not nobody at all 'cos all they'll do is snoop and stick their noses in. Nobody, I mean it, Miss. And it's not that bad, anyway. They'll take Dad away and I still love him and who'll look after us all then? Mum can't work with all the little ones to look after. They'll split us up and then we'll have to go into care and..."

She burst out crying and slumped down onto the bench as if exhausted and almost relieved by all the pent up emotion released.

Her story did not have a fairy tale ending even after many hours of deliberation and heart-rending on both sides in subsequent weeks.

Social services were not called in because Yvonne refused to talk to them and would not in any way implicate her father.

Mother was frightened and weary of everything and did not want to become involved in this latest episode in her seemingly sad life and the family did stay together for better or for worse.

Yvonne continued to come to school, just about maintaining her erratic attendance and presenting as a chastened character on the rare occasions she made it.

She got by, just.

"Are You Strong, Lass?"

Dear Mr and Mrs Stanton,

I am writing to express my sincere condolences for your recent sad loss. The entire teaching staff were extremely shocked to hear of the death of Stuart's brother-in-law, Private Ian Nixon, in the M62 coach bombing last week. It was a dreadful and senseless act and I think that, understandably, the whole country is still in a state of deep shock and revulsion.

It must have come as an enormous blow to the entire family. Stuart used to talk about Ian all the time and was very proud of him. As you are no doubt aware, he is hoping to pursue a career in the army himself which I suspect will cause some soul-searching in the family.

Please be assured that we are thinking about you in these very difficult times and you may have every confidence that we will keep an extra special eye out for Stuart's wellbeing. Do not hesitate to get in touch with the school if you think that there is any way we can help you further.

Yours sincerely
Stanley Cowburn
Headmaster

5.

`Yorkshire Regiment

Dear Miss,

Please can you explain to me why our Malcolm needs to get his hair cut again? I did take him just before school started and that's only a few weeks ago. He has now come home and said that the PE teacher says it is far too long and keeps flopping into his eyes. I think that that is just not true because I did give his fringe a bit of a trim only the other day.

Also doesn't the teacher know that it is fashionable to wear your hair longer these days? I think it's called the shag after that Jane Fonda film. He is not in the army and it's not the 1950s after all. I bet that Mr Miller is just jealous because he is going bald and getting very thin on top. Anyway, let me know what you think to the points of view that I have written, if you will. Thanking you.

Yours sincerely,
Diane Bell

AS in the classroom, the staff room can be a wary place for a newcomer, especially one seen as easy prey for those seeking diversion from a long and, often, disheartening week.

A core of the staff had come to the school around the same time and were a strong group so wet behind the ears incomers like me were fair game.

Varied fates had befallen my predecessor who had been appointed to the post temporarily.

She had been a quiet, slightly eccentric and unassuming lady by all accounts who had struggled to keep discipline in the classroom and had found it hard to hold her own in the staffroom as well.

She was teased mercilessly by the staff and pupils alike and even had her newspaper set on fire in the staff room as she was in the process of reading it. Her knitting wool was seized by some of the men and wound around every chair leg until the room resembled a maze, her shrieks of protest ignored and only serving to urge the perpetrators on.

Another staff room sport involved, predominantly, female legs being tied to chair legs with scarves, mainly by men, long before sexual harassment, rightly, became an issue.

Hearing such stories, I was determined not to get caught out, especially being one of the new-breed of graduate teachers whose worth had not been universally accepted by an inner city state school in the North of England.

John, the Rural Studies teacher and Alan, who took Metalwork, did not pay any homage to all the fancy didactic nonsense justifying their so called status.

And in many ways they were quite correct not to do.

I quickly learned that understanding the pupils and their background and keeping good order was equally important.

Poor old Vernon, who was then the only other graduate teacher on the staff at the time, and I were the butt of much teasing and many jokes and pranks.

However, we survived and, slowly, the attitude towards graduates did change and both sides co-existed in relative harmony.

There was an awful lot of inverted snobbery as well although I failed to recognise it at the time.

Some of the worst offenders were very blinkered, would not listen to alternative reason and could become quite confrontational.

Their way was the only one and if you had not completed two or three years at teacher training college then you had no business calling yourself a teacher.

Stanley Cowburn, the headmaster, was a character in his own right. Small and rounded, with a greying and thinning thatch, he was almost ready for retirement.

He'd been in charge of a school in another town which had closed down and frequently gave the impression that he was on the last lap.

He chose, on several occasions, to refer disciplinary problems to the deputy head or the senior master which sometimes caused a degree of friction, although his typically Yorkshire humour was never far from the surface.

Once, he had a mighty coughing and sneezing fit and lost his false teeth down the toilet just at the precise moment that an irate and somewhat flustered parent wanted to talk to him about her daughter.

But with typical grit he cracked a joke about it and dealt with the lady in question barely moving his mouth as he spoke earnestly to her. I seem to remember that Vernon and I were more impressed that the Headmaster actually had his very own toilet in his office than about anything else.

He was kind and a gentleman who meant well on most occasions but I'm not sure that he possessed the necessary drive and vision which the school needed at that particular time. Some of the more senior members of staff were dissatisfied with his lack of real leadership and I frequently heard mutterings to that effect in the staffroom and on the corridors.

The deputy headmistress, Miss Dorothy Margaret Brooke, was an absolute gem! She had been appointed to the post when the school opened about four years prior to my arrival and came with a wealth of skills and good recommendations.

About fifty years old, she was quite a frail looking character which belied her inner strengths and toughness.

She wore Harris Tweed skirts and pastel coloured blouses with bows at the neck, her feet clad in very sensible sturdy shoes from Earnshaws with which to pound the corridors at regular intervals, in order to stop trouble before it even started.

Apart from a little face powder and a touch of rouge, she didn't wear make-up although she was always followed by the aroma of Yardley's Lavender or Lily of the Valley.

Her hair was fairly short and wispy and swept back off her face in a matter of fact way, and when she needed to attend to anything up close, she would carefully pull out a pair of spectacles from her well-worn leather handbag and position them on the end of her nose.

So much warmth, experience, humour and efficiency was rarely found in a single package but DMB – as Miss Brooke was affectionately known – had it all in abundance.

"Are you strong, lass?" she asked me with piercing eyes and a wry smile when I arrived. "You'll need to be to work in this school, right enough."

She also possessed that most enviable talent which enabled her to weigh people up in a flash and was not impressed by paper qualifications or folk above their station.

It was her duty to give the pupils in her care the best possible opportunities and values, she wanted to teach them to try and live their lives honestly and purposefully.

She was a very religious lady but not one who insisted that everyone followed her creed, was a regular church goer and did lots of good work for various charities. She smoked Players cigarettes like a chimney, had orange nicotine stains on her fingers and coughed regularly and loudly.

"There's plenty in that graveyard that would be glad o' my cough!" she would remark frequently to casual observers, punctuating her remark with her trademark coughing.

In her study, on a bookcase and next to a battered looking ashtray, there stood an amazing wooden and metal contraption with a pulley and a coloured flag attached to it.

It seemed to loom large over the entire bookcase and Vernon and I would stare in amazement at it whenever we found ourselves in the office.

This contraption was, as DMB informed us, the device she used to celebrate those rare occasions when all the staff managed to make it into school.

She told us as on numerous subsequent occasions that some of the teachers were a somewhat feckless bunch, especially the men.

On those rare days when everyone made it in to school, the contraption was prominently displayed in the corridor outside the main office for all to admire.

As if to further make her point, she would wind the squeaky handle as hard as she could and then stood back in order to watch triumphantly as the flag staggered to the top. She didn't need to say another word.

The same cupboard which was the home of the flag also housed a bottle of the finest Harvey's Bristol Cream sherry.

It was Miss Brooke's special and rare brand of humour which allowed many of us to survive several situations which may well have seen off lesser beings,

Dry, apt and sometimes dark, it was never coarse.

Once, when a girl was collecting money for an Old Soldiers' charity, she knocked tentatively on Miss Brooke's door, rattling her tin as hard as she could.

Looking up through a fug of smoke and ash, DMB dropped a few coppers into the tin, at the same time asking the already embarrassed child if it would be possible for her to arrange a meeting with a young soldier never mind an old one.

The pupil, covered in embarrassment, shuffled out of the door as quickly as her little legs would carry her.

On those days when things were hectic and seemingly fruitless, you could often hear Miss Brooke utter one of her famous declarations that: "She didn't' know if she was on this earth or Fuller's."

She was also adept in any situation, no matter how incongruous.

One day in 1972 we were visited by American pop singer and songwriter Johnny Nash who was enjoying success in both the British and American charts with his song 'I Can See Clearly Now'.

For teenage kids – and staff – in an inner city Northern school on a wet, humid afternoon this was about as exotic and foreign as you could get.

Great excitement and puzzled anticipation could be felt during the morning leading up to his performance.

He sang his reggae-influenced song and several others

and was well received on the whole, a welcome diversion from double biology or history.

Miss Brooke, who was responsible for looking after him, behaved impeccably even though her music experiences and preferences were a million miles away from what she had just witnessed but from then on she used the title of his signature song with a mocking, dismissive or occasionally sarcastic air to continually reassure us all at staff meetings that things were going to be just fine.

The domestic science room, known affectionately as the Domsky, was a mystery to many of us on the teaching staff.

Mainly based around teaching cookery, it consisted of several large formica tables and work stations with stools placed around them from which the girls listened to the instructions and then prepared and cooked the food.

Boys were installed in the metalwork or woodwork workshops and never the twain did meet although the boys would hang around outside waiting for the girls to bring out their wares for them to taste.

The Domsky teachers were very strong characters and Valerie Skye, in particular, ruled with a rod of iron.

She was stout and a strong looking lady with dark brown hair and piercing brown eyes.

You did as you were told and never argued whether a member of staff or one of the girls and you certainly never ventured into the room unless you were invited.

Subsequently, I wondered if it was to avoid the sight of Mrs S and her sidekick, Freda Knight, apparently smoking and putting on their nail varnish while demonstrating how to mix up the ingredients for a perfect apple crumble.

Mrs Skye, in particular, liked a joke and was renowned for sending some poor unsuspecting girl to delve into every single cupboard in the room until she found a dish long enough to accommodate the sticks of fine Yorkshire rhubarb she was about to use to make a pie.

At the end of the school day, lots of girls could be seen carrying home their delicious smelling treats which were tucked away in their gondola wicker baskets covered over with a checked tea towel.

They had cooked them ready for Dad's tea and were, rightly, so proud of themselves mastering skills that would stand them in good stead for the rest of their lives.

Part of the domestic science room was an alcove referred to as 'the flat,' a corner separated off which was designed as a dining room.

There was a sideboard, dining table and chairs, wrought iron magazine rack, small armless chair which looked very uncomfortable and vases of artificial flowers.

The floor was covered in beige-coloured lino with a square of heavily patterned carpet in the middle of it.

Vernon and I were totally mystified at first when whispered exchanges at the staff room door were frequently overheard concerning use of the flat.

It later transpired that as you became an established member of staff, the fourth year girls might invite you to dinner with them in it.

I suspect that you had to be approved of by Mrs Skye in the first instance and eventually we were both invited on several occasions and enjoyed delicious fare and service.

Violet Land was an English teacher who had a complete mastery of the language and a vocabulary that an Army Sergeant Major would be proud to claim as his own.

She certainly made an impression on her first day, when early one morning in the staffroom, as I pushed the door open, I could hear expletives and the sound of shouting.

The voices rose higher and were joined by the sound of

breaking pottery. I edged myself tentatively into the room and peered somewhat apprehensively round the door and the image of a wild woman met my eyes.

The object of her wrath was poor old Mr Norris the physics teacher, who had apparently dared to ask her why she was using his coffee mug, one from Hornsea Pottery which he'd purchased on the school trip.

Her woolly blond hair cascaded across her forehead and down her back, she was wearing a tartan pinafore dress, dark green blouse adorned with a huge bow at the neck and knee length black leather boots.

She certainly ensured that everyone would remember her first day in school and never modified her behaviour throughout her time there, which admittedly wasn't very long.

She was a very good teacher by all accounts and got creditable exam results but was more instantly recognised for her histrionics.

I never met anyone quite like 'Dusty' Miller, one of the PE teachers.

His proper name was Derek and, despite his profession, was quite heavily built yet surprisingly very light on his feet.

His main sports were cricket, athletics and swimming at which he was particularly proficient.

He'd been at the school since it opened and spent all of his teaching career in the area and would have been in his early thirties when I first encountered him.

The kids openly referred to him by his nickname, he was very popular and spent a lot of time running after-school clubs and arranging coaching sessions in order to encourage pupils to make the most of their sporting abilities.

He knew that the cards were stacked heavily against

some of them and that they had a lot to contend with in their everyday life, so he tried to provide a different world for them in which they could excel, if only for a very short time.

In the staffroom, he really came into his own with his laid back attitude and dry sense of humour.

He could be extremely annoying and would claim not to understand what you wanted initially and would then burst out into loud guffaws of throaty laughter as you became more and more exasperated.

There were those among the teaching staff who were of the opinion that when he pretended not to understand, that it was simply because he really didn't. Indeed several colleagues thought he was not very bright or up to some of the demands made on him, a typical sports teacher.

He never had any money on him, citing no tracksuit had pockets and his wallet was always over in the PE office.

Indeed, I recall one time, when instead of putting some money in the collecting tin for a retiring colleague, he scooped a handful out saying that he needed it to pay Mrs Garside for his tea money.

Honest as the day is long, he always put it back but it did cause a few feathers to fly on several occasions although he could never see what the fuss was about. He just bumbled on regardless and rarely, if ever, took offence.

One very severe winter, the harsh conditions necessitated that the school was closed to pupils but the staff were expected to make every effort to get in.

This was an extremely rare event because in those days schools did not close at all unless the circumstances were absolutely dire. If the heating system wasn't working, then you just kept all your outdoor clothes on and coped.

The snow was heavy but most of the staff had managed to make it in and busied themselves with administrative tasks in the absence of pupils. At break time it had been deemed sensible to embark upon some serious snow clearing in the playground in order to ensure that our escape was ensured at the appropriate hour.

Gloves and scarves were donned, shovels found and shifting begun around the immediate area near the staff cars.

Many hands made light work and the job was completed in a relatively short period of time.

Just as the work party was about to make its way back indoors, the eagle-eyed art teacher noticed that one member of staff was very noticeable by his absence.

"Where is that bloody idle Dusty Miller? Why is he not out here with us lot shovelling, the lazy git!"

Someone pointed out that he was warmly ensconced in the staff room reading the *Yorkshire Post* and drinking tea.

She and some similarly incensed colleagues immediately turned back round and proceeded to redistribute the snow into heaps so that it completely trapped Dusty's Vauxhall.

"That'll show the slacker that we mean business! Bloody cheek! Who does he think he is?" she muttered under her breath as she made her way back inside, at the same time stifling a giggle.

When he eventually tried to get out I'm not sure he even realised that it was only his vehicle which was trapped.

Dusty consumed vast amounts of tea at all hours of the day, usually in other people's mugs and often free of charge because he was always at least two weeks behind with his tea money. When he had stirred and pummelled the teabag for the very last time and extracted the maximum goodness from it – he liked his tea really strong – he would abandon the sorry looking, soggy parcel wherever in the staffroom he happened to be at the time.

"Are You Strong, Lass?"

They could be found anywhere from desktops to chair arms, from register racks to mark books, rarely in the waste paper basket or in the specially designated receptacle placed conveniently on the edge of the draining board

That would infuriate a large number of staff who would voice their displeasure at every possible opportunity and try to make him see the error of his ways.

The art teacher was not a lady to be messed with and again came up with a plan to teach him a lesson.

The following morning, as Dusty made his way to the pigeonhole to collect his mail, she peered over the top of her newspaper with more than a passing interest than normal.

"Ooh, look, something interesting for once instead of the usual junk I get," exclaimed Dusty excitedly.

He reached up to the shelf and pulled down the small parcel which was protruding at an angle.

"I wonder what it can be? It's not my birthday for another month yet," he chortled.

Dusty began to tear off the Sellotape and brown paper from the parcel which was precariously balanced on top of his teaching materials.

As the wrapping fell away, a suspicious brown liquid began to seep out and drip all over his important papers and track suit sleeves.

It continued to ooze and squelch and the soggy brown mass finally gave up its precious cargo of about ten or so used and very wet teabags, which fell out rendering his notes virtually illegible.

Dusty did at least have the decency to blush as well as grin as he listened to the cheering cries of his colleagues.

It was one of the very rare times that I saw him even slightly embarrassed in his entire teaching career and, soon after, he developed a liking for coffee.

Dear Miss,

I don't make a habit of writing to school as you know, but our Tony has asked me to get in touch with you about his science homework. It is not his favourite subject but he had really set his stall out last night to do his best because we have promised him a bit extra at Christmas if he bucks his ideas up. He desperately wants a Spirograph, he says.

He had got all his stuff together to make this space rocket thing, cardboard boxes, two Creamola Foam tins, toilet roll holders, empty Stardrops bottles, tin foil, bits of string, glue etc and he had just got started when there was a power cut! Every single light went out along the electric bar heater and we couldn't find a torch.

He did wait a bit but after three hours, I told him to go to bed as he was getting cold and tired as well. He is really nattered that he'll be in trouble with that new woman science teacher.

Hoping you can sort it out. Our Tony says you will because you are like that and do what you say you will do.

Yours,
Rosalie Furniss

6.

Yorkshire Ridings and Beyond

Dear Miss,

We are really sorry to tell you but we will have to cancel our Philip's place on the school trip to Belgium in May next year.

Unfortunately, his Dad has been put on a three day working week at B.J.D. and we just don't have that sort of spare money. There is also a distinct possibility that he will lose his job eventually. Our Philip says that he will save all of his pocket money from his paper round but I know that it just won't work out. There is just too much uncertainty about money and jobs at the moment.

We are really sorry to have messed you about and hope perhaps that you might be able to consider him for a place on a trip in the future. He is very disappointed as you can imagine because he loves French and I can assure you that we have not taken the decision lightly.

We have never been abroad ourselves and we would like

Philip to have as many opportunities in life as possible to help him get on in the world.

Yours sincerely,
Martin and Sharon Lodge

I MUST have been completely mad to agree to take a school trip to France, aged only 23.

"Yes, Headmaster, of course I will, it'll be a great privilege and the children will get so much out of it."

I can still hear these words ringing in my head as they escaped carelessly from my mouth.

I was excited and flattered and I did see it as something of a challenge but I would be able to really bring my subject to life and share my enthusiasm with all these eager and receptive young minds.

Before attempting to structure my accompanying worksheets, I had to spend a good few sessions with Gerald who was the technician and a general Jack of all trades.

The Banda machine, which I had to learn to use to copy and duplicate, was a complete mystery to me. The Graduate Certificate in Education had certainly not prepared me for the joys of inky fingers, mysterious knobs and buttons and an evil smell.

My colleagues and I all worked together on the planning and the necessary parents' evenings as we attempted to field the inevitable awkward questions and tried to assume an air of total command and competence.

The kids were really giddy for weeks before the proposed departure date. Every French lesson began with a long list of questions, some of which they sought the answer to and some of which were used simply as a red herring in order to avoid the actual lesson.

I allayed fears in areas where I felt that I could and told

white lies in those where I had not the remotest idea of what I was talking about.

Then we all set about looking at the geographical area in France where we were going to stay.

We pored over atlases and travel books and stuck pins in relevant places, practised our conversational French and performed our role play situations in a wide variety of shops, cafes, restaurants and, inevitably, toilets.

All the children were logged and listed onto a joint passport, insurance forms were completed and payments made on a weekly basis into a school bank.

It was hard work and very new to me but I was very fortunate to have more experienced colleagues on hand to assist.

Little did I know, that was the easy part of the whole operation.

The trip was scheduled to leave during the half-term holiday in late May and we were booked onto an early morning ferry crossing from Dover to Calais and we assembled at school just before midnight ready for the coach journey.

The school looked even stranger at that ungodly hour than it did normally.

Thirty suitcases of all colours, sizes and varying degrees of wear and tear were lined up in the entrance hall, all neatly adorned with the labels provided by the travel company just as I had requested; so far, so good.

That was until I realised that at least ten of them carried the name Peter Smith, the name I'd used as an example when practising in class beforehand.

Spare ones were quickly found and parents were hurriedly asked to fill them in correctly for their loved ones.

Many of the children had not been out of Yorkshire

before, let alone on a ferry to a foreign country. People did not travel far in 1972 and horizons were very limited.

The era of relatively cheap and widely available package holidays by air was not yet upon us and there was little spare money available for travel of any sort.

Many of the parents had made great financial sacrifices in order to enable their offspring to go on this trip, anxious for them to enjoy an experience which had not been possible for them.

That was something which I took very much on board for this and subsequent ones, and I'd like to think that the advance planning and hard work resulted in something where the parents got good value for their money.

I felt a great responsibility that the trip should be a meaningful experience and one from which the children would derive real benefit.

I tried to make them aware of their surroundings and would point things out to them as we familiarised ourselves with our destination; I wanted them to remember their first visit to France as special.

Lots of them were predictably ill as they mixed chips, Wagon Wheels and Refreshers with the undulating waves of the Channel and I vividly remember standing in pools of vomit in the toilets, offering some sort of reassurance that if they put their head between their knees, stayed still and put an immediate stop to stuffing even more sweets into their mouths, then they would very soon begin to feel a little better.

After the long and rough crossing and what seemed like an even longer and more tiring coach journey through northern France, we finally arrived at the hotel on the Normandy coast that was to be our home for the next six days.

A frisson of excitement ran through the coach as we

parked up outside and then began unloading the suitcases and getting the rooms sorted out.

It was a relatively small establishment that was simply furnished and spotlessly clean.

In what seemed like no time at all, we were all assembled in the dining room ready and eager for the first foray into the real world of French life, food and drink.

In all honesty, the meals in the hotel were viewed with great suspicion. Poulet might well be chicken but, to them, it was still 'foreign muck' and nothing like the chicken they ate in England.

I shall never forget the look of sheer horror and amazement on Alan Pearson's face as he was presented with a bowl of steaming moules marinière; he had never even heard of mussels.

Understandably, the frites and the crusty baguettes went down very well and gradually the children became more adventurous.

They were very proud of themselves when they spoke in French to waiters and waitresses and several of them visibly grew in confidence as the week went on.

They went into cafés clutching their worksheets and ordered their drinks and snacks proudly, enjoying the interaction it created.

When they were out and about in the streets of the small French town where we were staying, they loved it when the shopkeepers engaged them and learned new aspects that they had hitherto only glimpsed in text books.

On one occasion, a lad called Gordon had ordered a lemonade and the bottle came bearing the label 'Pschitt.'

"Hey up Miss, look at this! I've only gone and got missen a bottle of shit," he shouted to much raucous laughter from his mates.

We completed our workbooks together, talked to the locals, climbed on tanks, visited the World War Two beaches, and the town of Caen with the amazing Bayeux Tapestry.

On a particularly hot day, we explored the narrow winding streets of a small town, the kids periodically popping into one of the many souvenir shops to look for trinkets to take back home as mementos.

Each child had been allowed to bring some French francs with them but there had been an upper limit placed of about £10-worth in order to preserve some sort of reason.

The money was kept in a 'bank' by a member of staff and given out in small amounts every day in order to try and avoid the money being lost or stolen.

Jackie Gibbons, whose mum and dad had a pub back home, could hardly conceal her delight when eyeing up a bracelet made of pebbles that cost 700 francs.

"I'm going to get that," she said, much to my amazement as she strode towards the boutique in whose window it glinted.

Not wanting to see her make a fool of herself in there, after a quick investigation, it transpired that the bank in England had made an error and given her ten times the amount that she should have had.

Because the notes looked very alike and were quickly secreted away in an envelope, nobody had spotted the error before the money had found its way into Jackie's hands and she was off to spend it.

I had to quickly contact the bank in England by telephone in order to alert them to their mistake and before Jackie ran up huge debts which neither she nor her parents could afford.

That was the easy part, it was much more of a struggle trying to explain it all to the young lady concerned who was of the opinion that if she had the money in her hand, then she was entitled to do what she liked with it.

She was eventually pacified and distracted by another member of staff who had fortunately spied a very similar pebble bracelet, without the jewels, for a lot less money.

We missed our mums, some of us tried to drink too much alcohol, made new friends and, before we knew it, it was time to pack up and come home.

One of my abiding memories was the almost deserted playground which awaited us on our return to school.

It was three o'clock in the morning and some of the pupils just got off the coach, collected their cases and disappeared into the night.

Nobody met them and even though they didn't have far to go, my husband was amazed, and could not really come to terms with the fact that some parents were happy for their youngsters to find their own way home at that time in the morning.

Trips became something to look forward to, although I hadn't realised how much that applied to those who became caught up in them and who sometimes got more than they bargained for. On one coach trip, my attention was attracted initially by peals of raucous laughter and much shrieking from the back seat and the subsequent loud hooting of horns as several lorries and vans sped by us.

The drivers were grinning and waving for all they were worth and I eventually discovered that the young ladies had decided to perform in a way where they could use their assets to the best possible advantage.

As a lorry appeared immediately behind the coach, school jumpers and blouses would be re-arranged accordingly. How there were not more pile-ups, I shall never know.

Then there was Clive Widdup part lovable rogue, part damn nuisance.

Small in stature, with a shock of curly blond hair, stub nose and very rosy cheeks, he gave the impression that butter would have struggled to melt in his mouth but appearances can be deceptive.

Because his older sister, Melissa, was as dull as ditch water, some people wrongly assumed that Clive was an easy going, mild-mannered lad who would do as he was told without a second thought.

However, a school trip to France provided him with the stage he needed to deliver his finest performance.

Ignoring all the rules and guidelines laid down well in advance, Clive decided to test the boundaries.

The big and very baggy blue woolly jumper, which he absolutely detested, that his mum had insisted on knitting for him to bring on the trip was indeed a godsend, but not in the way that Mrs Widdup had intended.

Underneath its ample proportions and vivid green stripes, Clive managed to secrete four or five cans of the local lager and smuggle them into the hotel where we were staying.

Once in his room, Clive proceeded to show off to his mates boasting about his daring escapades and inviting them to share in his liquid treasure.

However, they were either warier or less brave, and they feared the wrath of the teachers and subsequently their parents.

The others must have watched in some amusement and amazement as he commenced his Stella supper, downing one can after the other in rapid succession.

A gentle tap on my door about midnight revealed Philip Caxton who was worried about Clive's seeming comatose state after collapsing on his bunk drunk as a lord. After the initial laughter, the boys had become worried and I followed him back to their pungent room which hid an array of socks, pants, sweet wrappers, comics and other unmentionables which formed a huge mountain just behind the door.

On the bottom bunk lay Clive in his alcoholic near coma.

He was still fully clothed and snoring loudly. Fortunately, he hadn't been sick and so he was not in danger of choking.

The three other boys wondered, sheepishly, what to do next.

"He doesn't look very comfortable, does he?" I ventured, somewhat mischievously. "He really shouldn't have gone to bed in his best jumper and jeans, they'll get all creased and messed up which would be a shame."

They watched wide-eyed as I undressed him, removing his string vest and sweaty socks, leaving him in nothing but his pale blue Y-fronts.

Without saying a word I moved towards the door and bid goodnight to the open-mouthed audience.

"Sleep well, lads, and don't forget to remind Clive that we have a four hour coach journey tomorrow, followed by a long ferry crossing, poor weather forecast as well. I think it could be very rough."

Next morning, we packed up early to begin our long journey back home.

Clive was nowhere to be seen and when he did finally board the coach, looking very much the worse for wear, he gave me a funny look.

His skin looked even more sallow than normal and there were big dark circles under his bloodshot eyes.

Whilst there were whispers from his roommates, I never mentioned anything and he was far too embarrassed too and the drink incident went no further; I had all the ammunition I needed for his next misdemeanour and he knew it.

I bumped into Clive with his mother about a couple of months later in town. She chatted away to me, saying how much both Clive and his sister had enjoyed the trip.

He didn't say a word but remained pale and cowed at the side of his mother, quite a big lady, and I could read the words etched into his expression, 'please don't say anything, Miss.'

Dear Mr and Mrs Briggs

Thank you very much for your letter asking permission to take Wayne out of school for three days at the end of next week to go on holiday to Bridlington. Unfortunately, I regret to say that I am unable to grant this permission because of our school policy on holidays.

We do feel that it is very important for pupils to maintain a regular attendance in order to take full advantage of the many academic opportunities on offer at this school. Next week sees the beginning of intensive revision sessions in readiness for the GCE 'O' Level Examinations later on this term. I do hope you will understand that my decision has been made with Wayne's best interests at heart. He is a clever boy with a great deal of potential and we are expecting him to do very well in his examinations.

Please do not hesitate to get in touch with me should you have any questions and thank you in advance for your cooperation.

Yours sincerely,
Stanley Cowburn,
Headmaster

7.

A Yorkshire Rose

Dear Missus,

I would like to come up to school to talk to you in private sometime soon, please. It's a bit delicate. It's about our Jasmine. As you will have noticed she is quite a big girl.

She is getting really fed up of boys teasing her about her big bosoms.

Now, don't get me wrong. I know lads are lads because I have got one of my own to deal with. But there is a limit. She were right upset yesterday when she got home as some lad had shouted down the corridor for everybody to hear, "Blimey, you don't get many of them to t' pound!"

What made it even worse was that she was wearing her PE Aertex blouse which admittedly is a bit tight as I have not been able to get to the shops to buy her a bigger size yet.

There's nothing me or her Dad can do about it, but perhaps

*you can let me know a good time for me to come to school to talk
about it and see if we can sort something out.*

Yours sincerely,
Mrs L Wild [mother]

BRENDA had always been one of our more interesting and
colourful girls.

Regrettably, she always seemed to be a victim of other
people's actions and not her own, the product of a broken
home where desperation and despair ruled and allowed little
hope and happiness.

At fourteen, she was old beyond her years and had
never really had or enjoyed her own childhood.

She regularly looked after various younger siblings for
'our mam' and always made sure that they had the requisite
packet of salt and vinegar crisps and bottle of Cresta fizzy
pop for their breakfast.

She took them out in their pushchairs and wiped their
snotty noses, tolerated a succession of 'uncles' and frequently
skipped school to do the many chores and other tasks which
should really have been done by the adults in the family, had
there been any reliable ones.

Brenda's pathway in life was mapped out for her it
seemed and she didn't really have any say in the matter.

As a young teacher, I always found it very puzzling
that more experienced members of staff appeared to be
resigned to what the horizon held for girls like Brenda.

They accepted that they were powerless to do anything
about it as it was a no-win situation as far as they were
concerned. Home influences would always dominate.

At first I used to think that this was a very negative and
defeatist attitude but reluctantly, as time went on, I realised
that some problems were harder to solve than others and that

there was indeed a strong element of fate involved at many levels.

Inevitably, true to form and as if anxious to prove her critics correct, Brenda fell pregnant at fifteen owing to malfunctioning prevention.

Why she had chosen to become involved with the lad in question was not really clear and she probably did not know anyway, but often girls like her just wanted someone to love and care for them.

And if it resulted in a pregnancy, that was that, it was all treated with a certain inevitability.

The father, Alan the decorator, who was on a Youth Training Scheme, had come to 'our mam's' to slap some magnolia emulsion around but he had extended his skills outside of the kitchen area and into the bedroom and put in a bit of overtime as well.

Brenda had no intention of marrying him, she would probably never cast eyes on him again and didn't even like him.

But she went on to give birth and enjoyed looking after her son as well as she could, while still doing all the jobs for 'our mam.'

Education was over for Brenda before it had really started, as was the prospect of getting away from all the grief and strife which had plagued her young life.

Then, a year or two later, along came Ronnie, her new chap, a nice lad and former pupil; a bit older than Brenda but that didn't matter.

He worked for the Gas Board and he was not that bright, but he was a good sort and steady.

He'd marry Brenda, they would get a nice little council flat and she would have his tea on the table when he came home from work.

They would go to the seaside at Bank Holidays and eat Lyons Maid ice cream and play the slotties.

The benefits they could claim from the Social would come in handy as well because they would supplement Ronnie's modest wages.

It was Brenda's big adventure.

The date for the wedding was set at the local Registry Office, and a colleague and I were among the guests.

It was a fine but cold day with a bit of a breeze blowing, 'Our mam' was like a broody hen and the baby was the page boy.

He was now aged two and a bit and Brenda had bought him a posh little shirt with a bow tie and some green velvet trousers from the Littlewoods catalogue, 'the greatest name in postal shopping,' which she was paying off at 50p a week.

The bride herself was resplendent in a very tight-fitting creamy white embossed dress and she tottered dangerously on a pair of red embossed satin stilettos.

Cigarettes chain-smoked hurriedly round the back, the occasion began.

Brenda, her meringue-like dress billowing in all directions much to the amusement of the assembled, loved all the attention and basked in her moment of glory.

She was determined that she was going to make the best of all this and when it was finally time to go inside for the ceremony, Miners' very glossy lippy was re-applied, costumes and nylons were hitched up or rearranged and hats picked up from the ground where they rested.

Once inside the rather dull and foreboding Registry Office, Brenda got the giggles, the Best Man insisted on giving his opinion at the wrong time in loud stage whispers, 'our mam' coughed up years of phlegm and the page boy farted much to the great amusement of the assembled throng.

"Are You Strong, Lass?"

My colleague and I, who were sitting at the back of the room on two of the hardest wooden chairs desperately tried to keep straight faces as we surveyed the mounting chaos.

After what seemed like an eternity, Brenda and Ronnie were united in all that life was about to offer them.

There was a little bit of blushing, some giggling and smiling, a fair amount of swearing and enormous relief that it was all over.

There followed an awful lot of snogging, not least from old uncle Bert much to the disgust of the younger members of the wedding party.

Invitations had been sent out that people join the happy couple afterwards at the local hostelry but plans had had to be changed at the last minute because the landlord had run off with the bingo caller from the Empire Rooms down the road to whom Brenda's family were loosely related.

So at the last minute another venue had to be selected.

The honour fell to the aptly named Mucky Ferret pub which was not quite as good as the original choice but was all that was available at such short notice, and they did keep a good cellar.

There were pineapple and cheese cubes on sticks, firmly secured into a large grapefruit covered in silver foil, mushroom pasties, sausage rolls, sardine paste and potted meat sandwiches and Black Forest gateaux as well as plates groaning with fairy cakes and walnut whips.

We had only agreed to go to the ceremony to offer support to Brenda and as the group got ready to move on to the pub, I wondered what her life from here would be.

I wanted to believe that it would have a fairy tale ending and that she might get to live happily ever after with her prince in their palace.

She deserved some happiness in her short life and, in

some ways, marriage could have provided that security and worth that she so desperately craved – she didn't want much after all.

But it seldom happened that way.

Sadly, my fears were confirmed only a couple of years later when I bumped into her in town and it had all gone horribly wrong.

She and Ronnie were no longer together, he had moved out of the area, leaving her holding the baby.

She appeared surprisingly resilient and insisted on showing me what she had just bought for the toddler and the latest addition to the family.

She was laden with parcels which were hanging precariously on the pushchair handle and which contained very cheaply made frilly garments along with shiny unsuitable shoes for her.

Her eyes sparkled excitedly as she showed me them and, at the risk of undermining her pride in her purchases, I suggested that she might be better off buying good quality clothes from a charity shop.

A look of horror and revulsion spread across her face and she exclaimed at the top of her voice: "Nay Miss. Come off it! Am not 'avin' owt for mi babby that some other bugger's kid has worn, it 'as got to be best stuff."

I wasn't really surprised at her reaction and whilst I didn't agree with her reasoning, a large part of me applauded her aspiration.

I admired Brenda for following her heart, chasing her dreams and trying to do the right thing,

I still see her from time to time in town. She is a grandma now many times over and still has that resigned attitude to what she sees as her lot in life.

Still an enthusiastic smoker, in spite of several cancer

scares, she jogs on from day to day, helping her extended family in as many ways as she can.

She can't work, she tells me, and so has to rely on benefits and has hardly any money at all.

In spite of that, in the next breath, she informs me that she has arranged to buy a new puppy to stop her getting bored.

She still calls me 'Miss' and in my eyes she still seems young and vulnerable.

I'm pleased that I was invited to her nuptials all those years ago and that, perhaps, I have managed to have some small influence on her life, and that she remembers just a tiny bit of some of the advice and help we gave her.

Maybe, in her own way, she appreciated the input and concern that my colleagues and I showed all those years ago.

Dear Miss,

If our Christopher's jiggered in his classes today, it might be because we were all kept up all night long because the dog has had four puppies. There were two bitches and two dogs which is champion and they're all going on nicely!

We have some woman interested in buying them but we don't reckon much to her so we shall bide our time. We have to be sure that they go to a good home, you see, because otherwise it is not fair on the puppies and it is not just about the money.

If you think you might want a pup, just let on to our Christopher and we'll see what we can do for you.

Thank you,
Mrs H Stewart

8.

Yorkshire Lads and Lasses

Dear Miss,

*Please would you be so kind as to have a word with our Janine as
soon as you possibly can. She is determined to be a film star and
says she's off to do it whatever me and her dad say. She is only
fifteen, as you know, and has to do her CSEs next year.*

*We've always known well enough that she has a strong will
and she can be a bit of a madam but we are really getting a bit
concerned now. She seems dead set on it and nothing we say seems
to have any effect on her. We have even tried to get her uncle Jack
to talk to her because she worships the ground he walks on but not
even that has worked.*

*She says she wants to be like that actress Julie Christie
because she's seen her on posters and on the telly. Her bedroom wall
is covered with pictures of her and she is a member of her fan club.
We really are at our wits' end. What can we do about it? She could*

get a right good job in the local pet shop if she shaped herself and got shut of all her fancy, high and mighty ideas.

When I was at school, my dad wouldn't have even listened to me if I had talked such rubbish. Don't know where she gets it from but it certainly isn't on my side of the family. We would be very obliged if you could have a word. She likes you and we think she might listen.

Yours,
Mrs K L Pickard.

IT was just another long, boring lesson in an otherwise uneventful and tedious day for Maureen Copeland but for me it was a crucial milestone in my career.

Mr Burnside paid us a visit. He was a Local Authority Adviser whose role was to monitor and record the progress – or otherwise – of teachers who had recently been successful in passing their probationary year.

He was not an inspector, as such, but was certainly the nearest thing to one that I had ever encountered. To be fair, I had been warned of his impending visit and so had time to prepare my lesson thoroughly in the hope of impressing him.

Preparing turned out to be very different to implementing.

The day before, I made the class aware of the whys and the wherefores of his visit and I emphasised repeatedly that he was coming to observe me and that there was nothing for them to worry about.

Maureen just stared blankly at me as I was explaining all this, with a look of total bewilderment etched on her face.

I further reassured her that there was absolutely nothing for her to worry about and tried at the same time to block out the peal of warning bells that were chiming loudly inside my head.

Maureen liked to have her say and took no prisoners if she was in that mood. I reiterated that it was just a normal lesson for them; Mr Burnside would be sitting at the back of the classroom and essentially assessing what I did, not them.

Some of the kids thought that this was really funny and I sensed they were looking forward to it rather more than the normal French lesson.

I reminded them to be polite and to answer any questions that he might choose to ask them as sensibly and honestly as they could which almost ensured that they wouldn't.

We were about five minutes into the lesson when the door swung open and a thin wiry-looking man appeared.

He was middle aged but was balding rapidly. I rushed over to welcome him in, but he just motioned at me to move back to my desk and made his way to the isolated one which I had carefully placed at the back of the room.

As he did, one of the lads yelled out, "Hiya, mister! She's told us all about yer. Why were yer late? We get into right bother if we are."

"Andrew Dawson, sit down in your seat immediately and don't bother Mr Burnside with your silly chatter," I retorted as panic began to set in.

Once Mr Burnside had got himself as comfortable as a grown man can when seated at a school desk, I attempted to get the lesson started once again.

I'd planned a lesson which I thought would suit both the children and him and which would also allow me to show my very limited but slowly developing skills to the best possible advantage.

Although not particularly easy with a class of lower ability fourteen year olds, I had just given out vocabulary sheets and was about to start some basic explanations when, out of the corner of my eye, I was aware of the assessor getting up from his seat and making his way down the aisle between the desks, clipboard in hand.

I felt myself tightly gripping the edge of my desk as I monitored his short walk down the aisle and just managed to stifle a gasp of horror as he stopped exactly opposite Miss Maureen Copeland's.

He bent down and looked at her exercise book and grammar notes which, admittedly, were very neatly written but which were a complete mystery to her.

Mr Burnside picked the book up and flicked through it slowly and deliberately, pausing at certain pages and smiling weakly from time to time.

Finally, he found his voice, and said to Maureen, "Well I can see you are trying really hard my dear, and it is all very neat and well set out. Your handwriting is a credit to you."

Maureen thanked him and realised she had a captive audience, just the sort she liked. Without interruption, she proceeded to tell the official that her parents weren't too bothered about 'school stuff', preferring to use the family allowance on keeping the local afloat, take-outs of Watneys Red Barrel and huge cans of Party Seven.

I thought I was going to have a nervous breakdown there and then but just managed to flash Maureen a meaningful and threatening glare of disapproval.

Mr Burnside had the good grace to look bemused at best and mildly horrified at worst as he smiled weakly and shuffled off in the hope of finding a less forthright pupil.

June Spalding was only fifteen but had seen and seemingly done it all, her nefarious activities known by all on the estate. That accounted for her nickname, 'Martini.'

Like Maureen she was an outspoken young lady who had little, if any, regard for tact or appropriate behaviour in delicate situations, one of those girls that you really did not want to play any part whatsoever in a lesson where you were being observed.

But, once again, like a homing pigeon, my visitor decided that it was her opinion on my classroom strategies that would be best sought.

Ignoring his question, she immediately proceeded to tell him that her moniker was nothing to do with the alcoholic drink but the words of the advert that was prominent on telly at the time whose strapline was 'Any time, any place, anywhere.'

Before he could even register his shock, she continued that she was not bothered about exams because she could: "Earn her money in other ways...", before ending, somewhat provocatively with a toss of her pony tail.

Visits to the inner sanctum of the classroom were always a somewhat unknown quantity for all concerned.

More often than not the advisers and inspectors were there in a passive and observing role but sometimes the purpose of their visit was far from clear to a young teacher like me.

Some of them would simply sit quietly and scribble fervently as they absorbed the classroom activities, others would choose to play a more active part and engage the pupils in some sort of interaction and then, in retrospect, wished that they hadn't done so.

If the observer was a member of the Local Authority Advisory team then they often felt it incumbent upon them to instruct anyone and everyone.

I felt obliged to listen and automatically assumed that they must know what they were talking about but on several occasions thought to myself that some of what they said did not seem to make any sense at all.

Subsequent conversations with colleagues revealed similar insecurities and confusions.

One member of staff in the domestic science department related to me with sheer scorn and bitterness, an incident which had happened after one of her lesson observations.

Apparently, it had been suggested to her that she should enliven them by making them more 'pupil friendly' and instead of using eggs just to bake flans she should 'put on more of an engaging show' by throwing them high into the air first.

Fortunately for the assessor, the teacher was of a certain age or it would have been him tossed to the ceiling.

When I was teaching poetry to a very challenging class of fourteen year olds, I was heavily criticised for my choice of poem, 'Daffodils' by William Wordsworth.

How on earth did I expect 'children like these' to get any benefit from studying a poem so far removed from their realm of experience?

The assessor determined that it would be much more appropriate to select something which replicated their own often very grim and demanding lifestyles. Kitchen sink literature, I seem to recall it was entitled.

From somewhere, I found my young voice and pointed out that surely the sort of escapism and imagery at which Wordsworth excelled was much more likely to stimulate them than the mere repetition of the depressing and soul destroying situations in which they were already reluctant and imprisoned participants every day of their young lives.

She looked at me in an odd sort of way and did not choose to comment further. I remember feeling quite proud of myself.

One of the most delightful and rewarding classes I ever

taught was J1, a class of about twenty-five twelve and thirteen year olds. They were to be the first year group at the school to be entered for the General Certificate of Education examinations.

In 1971, it was my privilege to set them off on their four year journey to GCE French. It was an above average group of boys and girls from differing backgrounds but with one thing in common; they were of a similar standard and could, therefore, tackle the same type of academic issues and grammar questions with similar confidence.

It's fair to say that not all adored French but because it was deemed to be good to have a language qualification if they wanted to go to university, they at worst tolerated it.

They all tried hard most of the time and we had such fun as well. They loved the sense of achievement when they successfully tackled a demanding unseen translation or dictation.

Many of this group were the first to sign up for the school trips to France or bring things into school to form a French display.

At the end of their linguistic journey, the whole group was successful with everyone gaining a creditable pass and several achieving the highest grade.

I was so proud of them and even more gratified when several chose to carry on with the subject to 'A' level at the local college or at another city school which possessed a sixth form.

Those pupils were my first examination group and I have never forgotten them or their commitment to me and my subject in my early years of teaching; they made a big impression on me and were my inspiration.

Not all were so exemplary, some preferred to excel in name calling and fighting, especially the girls.

"Are You Strong, Lass?"

Elizabeth Glover, in particular, was always up for a good scrap, especially if there was an audience.

She delighted in them, they were part of her daily diet and one of the main reasons that she bothered to attend school at all.

There was usually no obvious reason for her pugilistic approach to life but she did seem to like the smell of blood.

On any given day someone in her favourite seat, who had taken the last ginger sponge at dinner time or just given what she deemed to be a 'mucky look' would become a victim.

She nearly always chose to pounce on her unsuspecting prey just outside the tuck shop where I was stationed.

It all seemed to erupt from nowhere and for no apparent reason. There was much spitting, hair pulling, scratching and kicking as well as the inevitable name calling, swearing and exchange of insults before she would launch herself mightily at and pin her unwilling opponent to the floor with the dexterity and brute force of an all-in wrestler.

The boys loved watching the girls fight, they would cheer raucously and urge them on and Elizabeth nearly always emerged triumphant and would boast about it for weeks afterwards.

I did try my best to pull them apart, threatening them, giving them stern looks and on some occasions, pleading with them.

More often than not it worked and I was grateful that I was not a mere scrap of a girl myself and that I was relatively strong.

As I employed all my resources and tried to physically pull them apart, Miss Brooke's words would ring round my head; "Are you strong, lass? You'll need to be to work in this school!"

If those combatants had known for just a split second how terrified and unsure of myself I was, they might still be scratching each other's eyes out now.

The accepted practice after such an incident was to arrange for the miscreants to attempt to write down their reasons for their behaviour and perhaps try to formulate some sort of apology.

Positioned at either end of the dining room at break time, out of grabbing and poking distance and under the watchful eye of the teacher on duty, they would reluctantly put pen to paper in order to record what had just transpired.

Bearing in mind that English was not perhaps their strongest subject, this exercise already had the hallmarks of disaster stamped across it.

Elizabeth's tended to be classics of their kind.

"I were just minding mi own business when she comes along, thinking she's queen o' corridors. Flouncing about as if she owns t' place. Well she do not! No way! And she needs to be reminded! She's only been in school ten minutes. All of a sudden she makes for me and raises 'er arm. Her face were all red and she looked proper cross. Then she goes and screams at me right in mi face. 'Yer fat cow, yer bag, yer better gerrout o mi way! I'm not scared on you so don't be thinking I am cos i'm not! and don't be thinkin' that the lad next door fancies you, cos he blummin' don't.' "So I goes, 'Who'd you think your talking to, clear off before I land you one and don't think ah don't mean it, cos ah do.'"

The other pugilist would have penned a similar account with a very different slant and the miscreants would duly hand over their completed scripts eyeing each other up with evil intent, all the while no doubt planning future confrontations, and then would both scuttle away to their respective classes.

"Are You Strong, Lass?"

We had many hilarious times in the staffroom when the scripts were read out at break by members of staff eager to practise their thespian skills.

For every Elizabeth Glover there was at least one quiet, unassuming child who desperately wanted to be part of the group but never would be.

Paul was a small and skinny lad for his age, whose shock of blond hair and an angelic face disguised many hidden problems.

He had no friends at all. He would try to buy and bribe his class with Spangles and sticks of 'spanish' which he had probably stolen or would plead with them in a sickly, ingratiating manner.

He'd follow them and offer to do errands but it was all to no avail. The other kids were not particularly nasty to him, they just couldn't be bothered and chose to ignore him.

He would have been totally invisible to them but for one thing, he absolutely stank.

Everywhere he went he left his tell-tale aroma behind him; on chairs, on the text books he had touched and on any PE kit that he had borrowed as he did not possess any of his own.

He was a victim in so many ways.

His mother was totally inadequate and his father long gone, he was neglected beyond belief and his basic needs ignored.

He rarely wore clean clothes and he was left to fend for himself at home while his mother went out drinking or to the bingo.

He was an only child so there were no elder siblings to look out for him and afford him some respite; he had a terrible life and endured unspeakable hardship.

The school was aware of his plight and helped where

104

it could but the wheels of officialdom moved exceedingly slowly.

I was amazed to discover that his form teacher kept a supply of underpants and socks in her desk drawer for him which she had bought with her own money.

Not many people knew about it because they didn't need to; it was done to try and alleviate some of Paul's embarrassment and misery.

Other teachers would buy items of kit for him, take them home and wash them and then keep them at school for future use rather than send them home with him where they would be lost.

I have never forgotten him or the bond I tried to forge with him.

I taught him French for two years before he was eventually taken into care. He enjoyed those lessons in as much as he ever enjoyed anything in life.

I tried to help him feel good about himself for just a little tiny fragment of time and took every opportunity to praise him.

But he had lost his childhood and he never got it back.

Subsequently, he spent a lot of time on the dole after drifting from one dead end job to another, got in with a bad lot and sought approval for the wrong sort of things.

He tried to look good and act big but was arrested for burglary and, with an almost predictable inevitability, was sent down.

It was written in his stars from an early age and I always felt sad that we, as teachers, could not do anything to prevent the outcome in spite of all the hard work and soul searching.

But the odds were stacked too much against him.

Cases like his made an enormous impression on me, I

had never come across such real hardship and was horrified by the implications and ramifications it brought in its wake.

I learned a lot from Paul's case and it stood me in good stead when I later became a head of year with several pastoral responsibilities, one of which involved liaising with outside agencies in an attempt to try and secure a decent deal for Philip.

He was thirteen years old and neglected in very similar ways as Paul had been.

One bitterly cold day in December, it had been arranged for a social worker to visit Philip's house with me to assess the suitability of the living conditions.

Nothing could have prepared me for the experience which followed. His mother was out, no doubt having been tipped off about our impending visit and the semi-detached council house looked as sad and neglected as its young inhabitant, stranded in the middle of a small garden which resembled a jungle.

Rubbish was strewn all over and the wooden panel of the front door had been kicked in with considerable force.

The gate was broken and swinging on its hinges and there was dog dirt and an old, battered dog bowl near the door.

We had been given a key but, in the event, didn't need it because the door was unlocked. Nevertheless we had to push very hard to gain access.

On the other side was the biggest pile of junk and rubbish that I had ever seen outside a council tip.

Empty Chum tins and baked bean cans, discarded beer and Woodpecker cider bottles, fish and chip papers and other types of detritus formed an immense mountain which reeked of rotting food and stale alcohol.

I was visibly taken aback but the social worker put a

reassuring hand on my arm and cast me a knowing glance which spoke volumes.

We ventured tentatively further in and the sight which awaited us in the kitchen was equally horrendous.

All the units were damaged, the tiles were smashed up and the floor was covered with yet more empty tins and bottles.

But it was an overpowering stench that stopped us in our tracks. We knew what it was and sure enough, in the far corner was the biggest pile of dog excrement you could imagine.

Closer examination of the other downstairs rooms provided similar distressing and sordid scenes.

Upstairs proved to be a similar scenario; smashed light fittings, torn wallpaper hanging off in long dangling strips, broken furniture and urine-soaked mattresses on which the poor kid was supposed to sleep.

It was not fit to house an animal, let alone a child.

The room was bitterly cold and smelled of damp and other inescapable odours. The only source of heat appeared at first to be a one bar tiny electric fire whose wire was damaged and which looked extremely dangerous.

On closer examination, however, I spotted what seemed to be a round scorch mark on the floorboards.

Seeing my bemused face, my colleague explained that it was probably the remnants of a coal fire which had been hurriedly and rather rashly lit in attempt to provide some sort of heat.

There was no grate or fireplace in sight and it was evident that the coal and paper had just been heaped up into a pile and a match put to it.

I wondered if I ought to view this as foolhardy and pathetic or a last desperate measure by a totally inadequate parent and how on earth could this happen in a civilised country in the 20th century?

The social worker had obviously seen it all before but to me it was a real eye opener and as we were leaving the property, she said to me in a low and very meaningful voice, "Always remember, dear, that you wipe your feet on the way out and not on the way in after a visit like that."

I have never forgotten the incident nor the comment.

The good news was that the mother was prosecuted and Philip placed with foster parents who helped him rebuild his shattered life somewhat.

He eventually secured a place on a Youth Training Scheme and became a bricklayer which allowed him to gain a little self-esteem.

The last I heard of him, he was married with two children and leading a meaningful life; in this particular case, the combined forces of school and outside agencies had enjoyed some success.

Dear Mr and Mrs Rawlinson,

Please find enclosed another copy of the letter which our Bobby brought home a couple of weeks ago regarding the class visit to the Museum in town next Wednesday. I understand from Bobby that the new puppy got hold of it and ate it and then, in his words, "Sicked it up all over the kitchen floor."

I should be obliged if you would fill in this new consent form and return it to school as soon as possible. Thank you for your cooperation in this matter.

Yours sincerely
Maureen Riley
Head of Year Four.

9.

Yorkshire Life

SEPTEMBER

Dear Miss,

Our Alan was not at school yesterday because we were flitting and I reckoned he was more use to me here than learning all that French. We had loads to pack up into our Colin's van and I have to say that our Alan was a right big help.

He isn't always but he was yesterday. He's much better at practical stuff like this than sitting in a classroom for hours on end. His Dad was just the same, it's just not his cup of tea at all.

He reckons that the only teacher who really understands him is Mr Cliff, that nice Chemistry teacher. He taught me and my brother years ago and everybody liked him. He was really approachable and he knew what he was talking about. He was brought up round here so he understands folk like us.

"Are You Strong, Lass?"

Alan does like you as his new teacher though because he has told me that he does. And he didn't have to say anything at all, did he?

Yours,

Mrs D Small

PS. I will get him a new pair of pumps as soon as I can. I know he is supposed to have them for the new term but Woolworths were shut when I popped down last night. By the way, can you give him back those Esso coins you took off him the other day? His grandpa has been collecting them from his filling station for ages and he wasn't right suited.

A NEW academic year meant new pencil cases, new uniforms, new teachers, new classes, new scrapes, new problems and new opportunities.

I loved September both as a child and a teacher. It seemed to represent a new start much more than the beginning of the calendar year in January.

I really enjoyed sorting out my pristine mark book and preparing the class lists in readiness, identifying my potential challenges, both positive and negative.

Fortunately, my initial September in school was not my first term, I'd been appointed three months earlier and so had some advantage over the wary new staff making their entry at precisely the same time as about one hundred new pupils.

I'd already been shown some of the ropes, along with ploys and strategies to help me survive, and I must confess to feeling just a little superior as I exchanged pleasantries with the nervous intake of colleagues.

On that first day back after the long summer away, there were a range of emotions on display as the pupils streamed down the drive in the twenty minutes or so before the school bell beckoned them in.

Some waved at the teachers, showing off their new

clothes and hairdos, others shrieked at the top of their voices as they desperately brought their mates up to date with their exploits whilst parted, whereas the reluctant bore the look of pained expression and boredom as they slunk reluctantly back to familiar incarceration for the next few weeks.

The first morning passed relatively calmly with the allocation of not for long, pristine text books and the welcoming of new pupils and staff at a special assembly.

The school smelled clean and fresh and looked at its best with a lick of paint here and there to spruce it up, matched by those who wandered around like peacocks in their brand new uniforms.

But for every swelled chest there were the less fortunate, dying a little inside from shame and embarrassment in ill-fitting hand me downs or well-worn, torn, dirty garments that couldn't afford to be replaced.

Even though they might not admit it, the majority of pupils were pleased to be back at school.

The long holidays were overrated and there was never enough money around for the kids to do what they really wanted.

Hours of playing in the quarries, going up town, chasing each other over the railway lines and sneaking into the pictures eventually lost their allure and they were ready once more to accept some structure and direction into their lives.

One September morning in my second year in teaching provided a life lesson for many of us.

We had been back at school about a couple of weeks and I was slowly getting acquainted with the pupils in my new registration group and, more importantly, their needs and idiosyncrasies.

Glenn Potter was a new lad whose family had recently

moved onto the estate from a socially deprived area in Leeds. It had been an uphill struggle for him to become accepted in an already established form group.

Throughout my career, I always felt very strongly about incomers and would impress on the class how important it was to make them feel welcome and involved; I saw it as a good opportunity to introduce pupils to the concept of empathy.

As well as having that particular mountain to climb, thirteen-year-old Glenn struggled with his school work and social skills.

But one isolated and well-timed incident, which had presented itself to him the previous weekend, managed to help him in his seemingly futile quest for acceptance and recognition by his peers.

Word had somehow got out that Glenn had been walking along the side of the canal on his way to town on the Saturday morning when he had seen a puppy struggling and splashing in the murky cold water, and yelping pitifully.

He'd immediately jumped in and succeeded in getting the distressed animal to the bank where he had wrapped it carefully in his jumper and rubbed it repeatedly until the poor creature showed signs of recovery.

As I took the register, I was aware that some of the class were chattering among themselves about the incident.

Glenn had reverted to type and wanted no part in the conversation and was sitting in a corner hunched up and reading *The Beano*, wishing he wasn't there.

"Glenn, put that comic down, will you, and pop out here, please," I said in order to break the increasing hum.

I had to repeat the request as his head was deeply immersed in the antics of Dennis the Menace but eventually, he reluctantly shuffled to the front of the room.

"I think it would be a good idea if you told the class exactly what happened to you at the weekend. In your own words and your own time, please," I requested of him.

He flashed me a look which was a mixture of surprise and blind panic.

"Aw Miss, do I 'ave to? They ain't that bothered, none of 'em," he mumbled awkwardly.

Despite his protestations, he positioned himself clumsily near the front of the room and rested his elbows on a desk, looking round almost expectantly.

I seized the chance, clapped my hands and said to the assembled throng, "Listen up everyone, Glenn has something he wants to tell us all."

After initial reluctance, they quietened down and stared at the unlikely storyteller, most with bored and indifferent expressions. However, the five minutes which followed were quite a revelation. It was just like that scene in *Kes*, only with a dog, not a kestrel.

After a somewhat shaky start, Glenn really came into his own and found his voice from somewhere.

He described, very movingly, how he had rescued the puppy, what he felt when he had seen it struggling in the water and how he had known what to do because he was interested in animals and had read lots of magazines and books he'd got from the library about them.

Ironically, it appeared almost effortless as he held their attention with his meaningful and helpful gestures, but more importantly because of the passion which accompanied his vivid description.

Without realising it, he had taken the first steps towards being accepted by his peers. Some of the class gathered round him after he had finished and asked him questions about the puppy and what he had done afterwards.

Glenn himself now had some currency with them and had acquitted himself with honour, he could begin to feel good about himself and take the small steps that would help him to build a more positive life at school.

I felt very emotional and was so proud of him; it was so good to see him glow with admittedly modest pride and feel as if he really belonged somewhere at last.

Autumn was also the time for Harvest Festivals. The children were asked to bring suitable contributions for baskets of fruit and vegetables to the hall for a special morning assembly and short dedication service to celebrate produce which came from the land.

I did blink more than once when two older lads crashed through the hall door, seconds before it was due to start, pushing an old wheelbarrow which was full of potatoes and apples.

It had started out as a dare and ended up as an accomplished feat.

The lads had apparently 'borrowed' the carrier from an old chap down at the allotment and helped him to solve his problem of a potato glut at the same time.

They had thrown in some carrots from their mums' kitchens and the waiting throng in the hall thought it was hilarious as we teachers quickly began a damage limitation exercise.

OCTOBER

Dear Mr and Mrs Swain,

I am writing to you specifically and personally about a matter concerning Geoffrey.

My letter is particularly relevant to you because of where you live, that is, in close proximity to Frederick House off Station Road. Apparently, last Thursday tea time, as Geoffrey was making his way home from school, there was a most unfortunate incident in which he sadly played a major role. One of the patients from Frederick House was minding his own business in their gardens when he was subjected to a totally unprovoked tirade of verbal abuse from your son and one of his friends.

The more upset and confused the poor man became, the more taunting and provocative your son acted, teasing him about Halloween and warning him to look out for ghouls and vampires. The fact that he was a vulnerable adult with severe mental disabilities seems to have completely escaped the boys' notice.

I cannot emphasise strongly enough how disappointed I am with this sort of behaviour which brings shame and disrepute on all concerned. The school will not tolerate such mindless actions and I have, of course written to the parents of the other boy.

I will be having severe words with them both and would be grateful if you would do the same and reinforce my grave concern; we must all learn to live side by side in harmony and tolerance. Thanking you in advance for your cooperation

Yours sincerely,
Mr Stanley Cowburn
Headmaster

THE upside of October was that there was a half term holiday in it, but there was still a very long way to go until Christmas! The Halloween disco and build up to it always provided incidents and an enjoyable level of ownership by the kids.

At that time no one was really sure what a disco was, the American word holding the promise of the exotic, but this was more of a regulated gathering usually held in the school hall because that was the most convenient large space.

It was also chosen because the dining room was next

door and crisps and soft drinks were made available for a very reasonable price.

On some occasions, a band was invited to perform and records would blast out, deafeningly, on the school's loudspeaker system, T. Rex's 'Bang a Gong (Get It On)', a particular floor filler.

The live artists tended to be recommendations from the kids who had a brother or friend of a friend trying to make their way in the burgeoning world of pop music and were happy to appear for a very modest sum.

Some of the more confident girls loved it when a group was on and would spend the whole set cavorting around the front of the stage shrieking loudly at the musicians, trying to attract their gaze and promising them varying dubious favours if they paid them the slightest bit of attention.

For most of them, the disco was also a fantastic opportunity for a fashion parade, an opportunity to wear that special outfit saved up for from Biba's or Dorothy P's.

The mini skirt was at its peak and it often seemed as if a competition was going on to see who could wear the shortest. As soon as the wearers left home the garments had been yanked up and twisted round with the aim of displaying as much bare flesh as possible, almost being worn as a belt, eliciting the expected comments and reactions from the admiring and offended.

For the Halloween disco, the hall was decked out with appropriate adornments from ghoulish figures to dangling skeletons, which lurked dangerously near the doors almost accosting those who made their way in and out.

Orange and black bunting and home-made flags were strung out behind the stage and along the back of the chairs in an attempt to rid the hall of its more usual utilitarian appearance.

Most had been made in the art lesson the day before or concocted with various odds and ends at dinner times during the preceding weeks.

All of that added to the fun and excitement on the night itself and because the kids rarely had such an opportunity to be part of and go to such events, they were determined to derive maximum benefit.

It was quite a modest affair, usually starting about six thirty in the evening and finishing about nine o'clock.

Groups of awkward adolescents would sprawl about on chair backs, occasionally venturing to dance or at least shuffle about on the floor, usually in a big group and with little chance of a romantic liaison even if any were that way inclined.

Any such cavorting, out of the prying eyes of teachers tended to take place on the way home in the alley round the back of the parade of shops in the shadow of the bus terminus.

Even though it was tame, it gave everyone the chance to either show off, play the fool, appear cool and 'with it', or impress in front of a captive audience and, generally, if not pushed too far, it was a good night out and a break from the norm.

There were the shy ones, lacking in confidence, who would huddle together in small groups and giggle nervously as the more raucous and forward of their contemporaries would cavort around on the dance floor and shout out obscenities or make lewd suggestions when the teachers' backs were turned.

The disco accentuated their vulnerability and awkwardness but for just a short period of time, it was good to escape from their mundane existence, step outside of the bubble and be part of the crowd.

Occasionally, the taunting, jeering and smirking threatened to boil over, as it did in the classroom, but the disco was a social highlight.

NOVEMBER

Dear Miss,

I am writing regarding Norma Kent who is in your class. Every Thursday, she goes to the Girl Guides at the Methodist Chapel in town and she has been presented with an award for her Nature collection. She really enjoys the meetings and gets a lot out of them.

I know she would really love to bring it into school so that the headmaster can present it to her again in assembly. She seems to think, however, that people will laugh and make fun of her and that it is not a suitable thing to be presented.

She doesn't know many other girls at the school who are in the Girl Guides and gets very flustered and easily upset.

I would be grateful if you could advise me of the best course of action and possibly have a word with her as well. She is getting worried about Bonfire Night because of that unfortunate incident with the firework last year; it really doesn't do her confidence any good at all.

Thanking you in advance.
George Faulkner (father)

BONFIRE Night – or 'Plot Neet' as it was known – was important in these parts but nothing compared to November the fourth.

Mischief Night was the evening when gangs of kids went out on the loose getting up to no good at all.

Growing up, the height of wickedness was to knock on someone's door or ring their doorbell and then scarper as fast as possible. Some went so far as to hide in a telephone box or even smear flour and water on its handle or dare to shout rude words from a safe distance behind a suitably positioned fence.

Once I'd become a teacher, Mischief Night took on a whole new and more menacing meaning.

I was never witness to any of the reported escapades first hand, hearing reports in the staff room or, if in earshot, gleefully from the miscreants themselves what they'd apparently got up to in a series of stage whispers for added effect.

Metal dustbin lids and fireworks inevitably were nearly always involved, especially as they could be bought individually to suit both intended victim and pocket.

Bangers, jumping crackers and Catherine wheels. Snowstorms, Golden Rains, Volcanoes, Roman Candles and Sparklers were prioritised in order of maximum impact and shaken within an inch of their lives to such an extent that it is a wonder any gunpowder was left in any of them.

Deafening explosions punctuated the hours of Mischief Night, accompanied by the piercing screams and terrified shouts of the girls at whom most of the unwelcome attention was directed.

The jumping crackers were particularly evil and potentially dangerous when tied to a dustbin lid, belt or bag.

Another big issue in the lead up to the fifth was the assiduous guarding of the bonfire which had been carefully and lovingly assembled during the previous couple of months when 'chumping' expeditions to gather wood and other combustibles had been undertaken.

There was a lot of rivalry between different factions on the estate as it was a matter of honour as to who could construct the biggest bonfire.

The deterring of marauding gangs who were intent on pillage and destruction was paramount and there were always many more than usual tired faces at school around the time.

This, coupled with the eager anticipation of what the evening held for them around the estate at the bonfire gatherings, invariably resulted in minds being elsewhere, eyes wandering out of the nearest available window at frequent intervals and very little meaningful work being completed.

The kids would chat all day long about what they were going to get up to, who they were going to scare out of their wits with jumping crackers and bangers, where they were going to place their milk bottles from which to launch their rockets and who was going to get the prize for eating the most potatoes and sausages cooked in the red hot cinders when the bonfire had died down.

On top of that there were parkin pigs and cinder toffee to devour when they got home.

Miraculously, I don't recall any bad accidents which was solely down to luck rather than having paid rapt attention in the safety sessions which we had organised for them all the preceding week.

On occasions we would also attempt to provide them with a historical perspective on the Gunpowder Plot and the local celebrity Guy Fawkes.

His legacy provided an opportunity for some of the estate children to demonstrate their budding entrepreneurial skills as they tirelessly paraded around the streets with their hurriedly constructed guy.

He was usually attired in whatever clothing they had managed to beg, borrow or steal and was propped up in some sort of a go cart or bogey with a piece of cardboard hurriedly slung round his neck inviting the locals to donate a penny.

If mild mannered requests didn't work, then veiled threats and blackmail were sometimes employed in order to squeeze as much out of the passers-by as possible.

DECEMBER

Dear Mr and Mrs Mitchell,

I am writing to you with regard to a serious incident concerning Barry and some other Third Year boys. As you are aware, this recent bout of snowy weather has caused numerous problems both inside and outside school; the staff have had an even more difficult job than normal trying to ensure that the school has run smoothly.

Last Thursday, 30th November, it transpires that there was a lot of trouble outside the Old People's Home on Ryton Road. Your son, along with several others, was caught throwing snowballs at the windows and, in some cases, at the residents themselves.

I am sure that you will be in complete agreement with me that that this sort of behaviour is totally unacceptable and not at all what we expect from our pupils. To compound the situation, Barry was extremely abusive when asked to curb his antisocial behaviour and his use of bad language was, quite frankly, disgusting.

We will not tolerate such disrespectful behaviour and I would very much appreciate it if you would make an appointment with my secretary in order that we might decide upon the next course of action.

Thank you in advance for your cooperation.

Yours sincerely,
Stanley Cowburn
Headmaster

"Are You Strong, Lass?"

I ALWAYS loved December in school, participating in festive activities with an abundance of young people all wanting to bring their own interpretation to this most special of seasons; I love Christmas with a passion.

I used to feel a moral duty to provide a child with a 'good deal' at this time of year simply because teachers and other key figures in my life had done the same for me years ago.

My first Christmas in school was extra special. I loved all the preparations, excitement and anticipation which punctuated the weeks running up to the end of term.

Activities in French lessons naturally became very Christmas orientated. It was good to deviate from the usual format and provided a welcome change of focus for some of those who struggled with concentration at the best of times.

French habits and customs were researched and the results compared and contrasted with the more familiar British patterns and trends.

We learned about Noël and the bûche de Noël and how Saint Nicholas played his part in the festivities as early as the 6th December.

Some of them were amazed that New Year was celebrated more than Christmas itself but the majority were prepared to listen and learn about different sorts of Christmases especially if it involved tasting samples.

On occasions I would take French chocolates and biscuits into school for us all to enjoy and we would quench our thirst with blackcurrant squash which we pretended was the finest vin rouge – it beat conjugating verbs for them.

It was in my second year of teaching when I decided to attempt to teach one of my first year classes of eleven and twelve year olds a French carol.

They were a good group of kids, very lively and always

up for a bit of a laugh and lots of mischief. Some of the other staff thought that I had taken total leave of my senses but an ever present stubborn streak chose to ignore the sceptics and press on regardless.

The carol I selected was entitled, 'Il est né, le Divin Enfant'. It had a catchy tune and seemed neither too long nor too complicated for the children to master.

We practised and practised the three verses and chorus, worked on our pronunciation, lost our tempers, found them again and eventually reached a point where we could just possibly risk going public.

As the days went by, a sense of real achievement was evident and there was a feeling of great pride in what they had managed to learn.

But the next step was the big one; standing on a stage in front of all your mates and the hard cases from the year above, and actually singing was bad enough but doing it all in French was bordering on ridiculous.

But there was one more cast of the die which I had hung on to for as long as I could; what I had not revealed to them until a little later was that we were also to form part of a large regional choir which was scheduled to perform at Leeds Town Hall just before Christmas.

After the initial panic and the establishing of a few ground rules, they embraced the whole enterprise with admirable enthusiasm and an almost reckless spirit.

The bus was booked, white shirts and blouses ironed within an inch of their lives, shoes polished, last minute rehearsals arranged and off we went, even leaving the Rolos, Munchies and Barretts' Sherbet Fountains at home so that our faces would remain as clean and scrubbed as they did when we set off.

It was a memorable experience for all the right reasons.

They behaved in the most exemplary fashion and did themselves and the school proud.

They thoroughly enjoyed the experience as did the handful of parents who had been able to accompany them as spectators.

Even some of the staff who had expressed some cynicism initially, gracefully acknowledged that it had been a good occasion and that the pupils had acquitted themselves with honour especially when the enormity of the situation finally hit them as they were overwhelmed and awestruck by the grandeur of Leeds Town Hall.

Also on stage that night was a pupil from our school who played the trumpet in a local brass band.

On this particular evening, he performed a solo, delivering his rendition with a great deal of aplomb which belied his tender years.

What was even more amazing was that Peter was a Thalidomide baby and had been born with deformed right arm.

He had not allowed his disability to thwart his musical ambitions and went on to even greater things as he grew older.

More often than not, snow was a big part of school life in December and the advent of the white stuff was guaranteed to wreak maximum havoc.

Whatever their age, kids greeted its blanketing outside the classroom window with glee especially the first fall of winter which invariably meant a stampede to the windows, knocking over desks and anything else which impeded their view.

At the best it meant the possibility of blocked roads and some unexpected days off although almost all lived within walking distance and schools tended to stay open regardless.

For the younger ones there was the prospect of building snowmen or sledging whilst the older ones were already forming gangs for vicious snowball fights, ramming it down poor unsuspecting souls' necks.

As a teacher, you just had to get used to this annual pantomime.

Depending upon the group, adaptations and modifications to the lesson could sometimes be employed in an attempt to use it as part of the learning.

Poems about snow, Allan Ahlberg's always a favourite, French weather forecasts, mathematical graphs showing snowfall ratios and historical facts tracking the effect of it in crucial battles but nothing could match the excitement of being out in it for the kids.

In spite of its frequent inclement weather, December was also a month well known for its sporting fixtures.

I was invited by the senior master to take charge of the under 13s hockey team, which involved arranging and coordinating fixtures and accompanying them to the various venues.

I saw it as a challenge and it helped me to establish myself early on in my career. You get to know children much better the more you have to do with them outside the classroom and it works the other way round as well.

They tend to see you through very different eyes and realise you're a human being not merely a demanding teacher.

It also fell to my lot to organise practice sessions in the dinner hour, select teams and find fixtures to play both after school and on Saturday mornings.

The grand culmination was an area tournament held on the first Saturday in December attended by all the local secondary schools, both state and private.

"Are You Strong, Lass?"

The event was scheduled to be held at the local, direct grant Girls' High School, to which scholarships were available to local pupils from all backgrounds, and the successful candidates had all their fees paid by the local educational authority.

IN my first year, I remember four boys and girls being successful in their applications and transferring from our school at the end of their first year.

Their achievements received very mixed reactions.

It was unknown territory for everyone and as such was viewed with a certain amount of fear peppered with mistrust.

Game day dawned, cold but fine, and the girls were at the prearranged meeting place bang on time, keenly chattering among themselves and in eager anticipation of what promised to be an exciting and challenging day ahead. They were all smartly dressed in school uniform, and had not only their hockey kit and boots stashed away in their bags, but also their post-match 'snap' in Tupperware containers.

The tournament went well and although we didn't win, we undoubtedly acquitted ourselves with honour and played to the very best of our ability.

For me, however, the discussions on the way home were to prove the most enlightening part of the event and, I like to think, became part of a learning curve for the girls.

"Well, I think we did very well to come where we did," commented Sheila in a matter of fact way.

"Yeah, dead right we did. They've got loads more kit and equipment to practise with than we have," observed Gillian.

"Did you see how many of them had those Junior Driver sticks? I'd kill for one of them," muttered Diane enviously.

"That's because they're rich. I bet they think we are a right load of upstarts, living on handouts and just managing to scrape by," retorted Judy with a defiant toss of her pony tail.

Beverley added in support of her increasingly indignant friends, "Yes, you're dead right. One of them gave me a right mucky look when I got the ball off her in a tackle."

I listened with interest initially as they made no attempt to hide their comments from me or disguise them in any way.

There was a brutal and innocent honesty in their declarations but in the interests of fairness and balance, I felt that I had to intervene.

We talked about inverted snobbery, over-simplifications and generalisations. I tried to encourage them to see all sides of the argument and assured them that the majority of the girls were just like them in the main and there would always be judgemental and vindictive people in all walks of life, including theirs.

It was very difficult trying to make them see reason and to help them adopt a more mature attitude, they were young and things were very much black and white for them.

But they took on board some of the points raised and it helped to give them a more balanced view of life in general.

JANUARY

Dear Missus,

We do not go to church. Never have and never will. What other folk do is up to them and we are not really bothered about them.

So what I want to know is why our Dawn has to take part in all the R.S., R.E., R.I. or S.K. lessons.

They are all telling her things that we do not want her to know about and all that mumbo jumbo about religion. We do not believe in any of it and we do not want her to have any part in the lessons. How do you know that what it says in the Bible is right?

So please can you sort it out and fix it so that our Dawn does not have to go to them any longer. She could catch up with some extra work if you like, I am sure that it would be more use to her, anyway.

Hoping you understand where we are coming from in this matter. We are not that suited that she has to go into assembly every day either, but I expect that we will just have to put up with that.

Thank you.
Brenda Oldham

THE first day back after the Christmas holidays was always somewhat challenging. When they were at junior and infant school, kids would have been happy to talk to their hearts' content about presents, Father Christmas, trips to see relatives and visits to Santa's Grotto.

But at High School things were very different. Huddled groups could be seen and heard discussing the various escapades and adventures they'd experienced during the holidays.

Darren's grandma had been up in court for being drunk and disorderly outside the Mucky Ferret pub on New Year's Eve; Tracey Barnes had been in a big scrap with Melanie Armstrong from next door all over a big bunch of mistletoe and a lad called Alan (who wasn't really interested in either of them); and Jason Cotton's mother had been caught necking whiskey in that new Tesco near the big roundabout.

Most were glad to be back at school if only to entertain their peers with such tales as debate in lessons turned to New Year resolutions in the home.

Somebody's mother had resolved not to have any more "bloody kids" because the four she had already were driving her round the bend. Someone else's dad had decided not to waste as much money on Christmas the following year and that he would rather have his teeth pulled out one by one than buy something on the 'never, never' again.

Kerry Collins was a girl from a troubled background who had been taken into care at the age of thirteen and placed in a children's home in the city.

Her background was troubled and disturbing and it had been decided that she would stand a better chance of success in life (whatever that might have meant to her) if she were to be placed in a more structured and safe environment.

Things had worked out quite well at first and she had managed to tame her temper and some of her aggression and cooperate with the staff who were trying their very best to help her settle in and establish some sort of normality.

However, as in so many cases like that of Kerry, the novelty wore off and her confusion and insecurity caused her to present as difficult, truculent and ungrateful.

The outcome was eventually that she was deemed unsuitable for that particular establishment and steps were put in place to arrange for Kerry to be admitted to another home at the end of the month.

She arrived at school on a freezing January morning looking even more downcast than she normally did. She'd had a huge argument with one of the members of staff at the home, told her where to go in no uncertain terms, questioned her parentage several times and tipped a bowl of cornflakes over her head. There was no way on earth that she was going back to that place after school and that was that.

I found myself listening once again to this poor lass's tale of woe.

I'd become quite fond of her and had tried to search beneath her aggressive exterior for some softer character traits, and they were there.

She trusted me and I just felt that she needed a chance, after all; it must have been very difficult for her to love or care for anyone else if she had not experienced it.

I approached the Deputy Head and, after a little negotiation, it was agreed that Kerry would spend the night at my house in order to allow things to calm down a little at the care home and give her the chance to think and reflect upon her behaviour.

It seemed to work and she was grateful for our intervention, a positive start to the calendar year for us both.

FEBRUARY

Dear Mrs Padgett,

As you are already aware, our Peter was invited to sit the entrance examination for the Grammar School last month because of his hard work and commitment.

We were really proud that the teachers thought that he might stand a chance and I am delighted to tell you that we received a letter yesterday morning saying that he had won a scholarship. He is to start in September.

We are obviously delighted that he has been given a place but understandably he is a little anxious about moving schools. It is, after all, a very big step.

He doesn't want people to think he is getting ideas above his station or that he will become a snob when he goes to the posh school.

We would be grateful if you could have a word with him just to help calm his fears and explain to him a little about what life at the Grammar School might involve. We both feel a bit at sea about it all to be honest.

We understand that this Direct Grant Scheme is very good and we do realise how lucky we are to be able to benefit from it. We would never have been able to afford to send him to such a school otherwise.

We have been told that this might be the last year that the scheme operates which would be a great shame. We are so pleased that he has got in just in time.

We'd also like to thank you and all the other teachers for all the help and encouragement that has been given to him. We have also written to the Headmaster to thank him.

Yours sincerely,
Kenneth and Judith Spears

FEBRUARY was the month of cold weather outside school and frequently miserable faces and moods to match inside.

It really was a battle royal to keep the kids' attention. They were welded to their coats and would insist on wearing gloves when asked to put pen to paper.

The bad weather regularly interfered with break times and they were often trapped inside, getting up to no good and parading around like caged animals or poring over *Jackie, Valentine, Beezer* or *Whizzer and Chips* – 'Two comics in one, double the fun.'

One of the key dates in the February calendar was Valentine's Day. On February 14th romance, or more often than not lust, was in the air.

Popular sweets Love Hearts were passed surreptitiously from admirer to the object of their affection, the messages engraved upon them eagerly read and then devoured, among them BE MINE, THRILL ME, LUSH LIPS and EVER TRUE

The biggest rogue in the fourth form arranged for a huge bunch of red roses to be delivered to school for his girlfriend.

He did get some stick about it but didn't care and stuck to his guns ignoring the cutting comments of his mates.

Shaun would have done anything for his Alison. In fact he shouted it from the rooftops as well as decorating walls, desks, text books and exercise books with his declarations of love; 'Shaun 4 Alison, 2getha, 4eva, 2stay!'

The motto was inscribed inside a hastily drawn heart shape written in either red Bic pen, blackboard chalk, fountain pen and on one memorable occasion bright green paint.

It obviously worked because they eventually got married and had a family.

February was also the month of my birthday and when it fell during term time, hurriedly-made cards and makeshift presents would appear on the desk whilst eager little faces watched in anticipation as they were opened.

I remember a lovely card signed by all the class which they had made at play time from all sorts of bits and bobs that they'd managed to beg, steal or borrow at short notice.

It beat the latex rubber whoopee cushion hidden in just the right position on my chair, a supposed gift from another class, but meant well.

One of my most poignant birthday memories happened during my first full year of teaching in 1972.

I had a first year class for French, period three just after morning break.

They were a nice enough group, very keen and eager to do well but not always fully motivated or well-behaved.

I was late arriving to the class because a parent had called to see me and it had been difficult to bring the conversation to an end without appearing rude. When I finally did arrive at the classroom door, I was aware of some scuffling at the other side.

I pushed the door open and swept in trying to look as important as a young new graduate teacher could.

"You boys get back to your places immediately or there will be trouble!" I shouted.

"Miss, Miss, Peter and Gary are in the storeroom," shrieked Maria Land, who would have shopped her own grandma for a bag of Rainbow Crystals and a bottle of dandelion and burdock.

I poked my head cautiously round the corner and there, sure enough, were the two miscreants, shuffling around awkwardly.

"Come out at once," I exclaimed. "What are you doing in there? You know the rules. I thought I could trust you two boys to do as you have been told, I'm very disappointed in you," I thundered going redder in the face as I was delivering the tirade.

Just as I was about to remonstrate further with them, Peter pulled something from behind his back and thrust it at me with a great sense of urgency.

I was taken aback but I just managed to regain my composure as I realised that it was a present.

They had obviously hidden it in the storeroom and were retrieving it when their enterprise had been cut short.

I looked at the somewhat crumpled parcel which I was now holding in my hand, wrapped in bright red shiny paper to match my face and held together with fluorescent silver ribbon.

The class crowded round in eager anticipation as I clumsily tried to undo the ribbon and inside was an ornate pink glass bottle filled with a mysterious liquid called, Coty

L'Aimant. Peter and Gary had nervously followed my every move and eagerly awaited my reaction.

"Boys," I said. "This is so kind of you but you shouldn't waste your money on me."

"We got it especially for you, Miss. It's proper French you know," muttered Gary blushing and shuffling his feet awkwardly.

"I can see that Gary, and I am really touched that you thought about me, it was a really nice thing to do."

"That's all right, Miss," Peter chipped in. "And we got a bit of money off it 'cos Gary's sister works in Boots on Saturdays."

The rest of the class did not quite know what to do, so they yelled three cheers loudly and somewhat raucously and then made their way reluctantly back to their seats.

With some sort of order restored, I began to try and share the joys of verb endings with them but by the time books had been given out, the end of the lesson was upon us.

I have never forgotten that act of generosity.

MARCH

Dear Miss,

As you know I do not write letters to school very often. We are normally both quite happy for you all to get on with the job of teaching our children.

However, Marlene came home really upset yesterday and when we finally got to the bottom of it all, it turns out that Mr Earl, the new English teacher, took her Jackie comic off her in the lesson.

Normally we would support the teacher's action and we agree that she should have been concentrating on her work, but apparently this particular copy is a special one.

David Cassidy, who she adores, features on the front cover and it gives all the details of his UK tour. I was wondering if you could have a quick word with Mr Earl and explain the situation to him.

We think that it would be better coming from you. Sorry to bother you but I am sure that you will appreciate how important these things are when you are twelve years old.

That Jackie *comic means the world to her. It's like her Bible.*

Yours sincerely,
Freda Massey

MARCH saw Fat Beryl's birthday.

She wasn't particularly popular but her dad was a manager at Lyons Bakery and had access to lots of samples and seconds.

He would bring his van into school on the appointed day, screeching down the drive with Fat Beryl in the front and jam rolls, sponge cakes and chocolate Swiss Rolls in trays in the back.

Cheers rang out as he unloaded his wares and several lads would be persuaded to carry them into the classroom ready for celebrations at morning break which couldn't come quickly enough.

Hordes of expectant, sweaty and very hungry boys crashed through the corridors, hoping to be the first to arrive at the impromptu party.

Beryl stood like Helen of Troy at the classroom door and welcomed the lads in, acknowledging their monosyllabic grunts gratefully because she knew that the following day everything would be back to normal.

It was her highlight in an otherwise drab and mundane existence.

"Are You Strong, Lass?"

APRIL

Dear Teacher,

I'm really sorry but we can't look after the school gerbil over the Easter holidays even though our Geoffrey told you we could. He can be such a silly boy sometimes.

His granny is coming to stay with us for a couple of weeks and she can't be doing with anything like that. She reckons that she's allergic.

There is no telling what she might do to it and I don't want all the bother, I have enough on at the moment.

Our Geoffrey had no business telling you we'd have it and I'm sorry to mess you about. Hope you can get somebody else to take care of it, we wouldn't wish it to come to any harm.

Obliged,
Mrs H Tranter

DUE to the vagaries of Easter, April would often see an end of term which was a very significant one for some of the older pupils.

They belonged to a group who were allowed to forsake their studies and make a brave attempt to enter the world of employment instead of taking exams.

Some of them did return to school to sit the odd one to complete their qualifications but for the vast majority it was the escape tunnel they had been digging away at for years.

They counted down for weeks beforehand which rendered many lessons more difficult to manage than usual.

In theory, they had to have a job to go to, something prearranged of which the school was aware but it wasn't always the case.

Casual jobs like milk and paper rounds were

sometimes included and often a seasonal one in a shop or on the market, which would only last a few weeks before being terminated.

That was a bitter pill for them because they'd been wooed and paid a paltry amount of money for doing a lot of donkey work and being a general dogsbody.

The kids were initially flattered and grateful to have some money and wrongly-perceived status while the bosses had easy access to a cheap and uncomplaining work force when they needed it most.

It was only when their work commitments were terminated unexpectedly and unfairly that the harsh world of unemployment rapidly became a reality and some of them would drift back to school at break times to chat to teachers about their next move.

Others would just hang around at the top of the drive, yelling to their mates, pretending to be cool and showing off but realising that the possible support network they had readily rejected was what they now really needed.

A particularly large and raucous throng clustered at the top of the drive and caught my attention one day whilst I was walking through the playground.

About a dozen or so lads had gathered and were listening intently as Martin Armstrong regaled them with his stories of daring deeds and his transformed and action packed life since he had said farewell to 'all that school rubbish.'

He had been taken on as an apprentice decorator by a local firm and had managed to survive for two weeks without getting the sack – much to everyone's great surprise.

Martin had been one of our characters and had just about survived his five years with us.

He was not without ability but, like so many others,

he'd not always chosen to use it wisely and had delighted in playing the class clown at every possible opportunity.

Nobody in his family had displayed an interest in any sort of further education so it went without saying that Martin would escape the shackles of the classroom as soon as he could and had joined the group of Easter leavers.

He'd taken time out of his dinner hour to come and show off at the school gate and inform anyone who would listen that he had now acquired grown up status and was no longer a kid like them.

He was in the world of work and he was getting a wage packet as well. The lads listened intently, some of them hanging on his every word.

Martin had just taken a break from his oration to light up a Player's No.6 when Gordon Warburton, who had been Martin's rival and arch enemy throughout school, and who had known him since he was four years old piped up, "But 'ave yer told 'em what 'appened last week? Our lass's boyfriend 'eard all about it from Michael Burton's brother."

It soon transpired that whereas Martin had settled in well in certain areas of the job, he had irritated several of the older apprentices who had very quickly become bored and annoyed by his tedious and constant chattering and joking at inappropriate times.

He had got away with it at school, often pushing teachers to the limit and simply ignoring his fellow classmates.

However, he was in a very different arena now; no excuses made for him, no backing down of young and inexperienced teachers or dominance over weaker brethren.

He had been dealt with in a way that was thought to be both effective and fitting. Four of the older apprentices had grabbed him as he was eating of his dinner, bundled him into the back of an old warehouse nearby and thrown him full length into an old cast iron bath full of whitewash.

They had then proceeded to ram a very large paintbrush into his wide-open mouth and make him promise by nodding mechanically that he would put a stop to his previous habits and give his voice a long overdue rest.

Unlike Christmas, the pupils struggled to see the religious significance of Easter, it was more about hiding, swapping, purloining or, occasionally, sharing chocolate for the vast majority. But when April 1st fell in term time, it was an ideal opportunity for high jinks and mischief.

Strategies varied, innocent tricks like calling the wrong names out or telling someone that there was something undesirable on their chair were interspersed with braver and more enterprising jaunts.

Teachers were not exempt either. I vividly remember turning round somewhat awkwardly and embarrassingly to check if I had a ladder in my nylons, Kayser Bondor and a present from my Auntie Kathleen, after some lad had suggested that I might have.

Eric Shepherd in K2 was a nice little lad who liked to hang out with the older boys and feel part of their gang and antics. He wasn't totally naive but neither was he street-wise and he certainly wasn't the sharpest knife in the box.

He suffered a lot because his Mum worked at the Co-op which labelled him with the nickname 'divi' but because he near-worshipped the lads in the older classes, they tolerated him as he was a useful errand runner or butt of their numerous, often dubious, escapades.

Peter Salter, who was the godfather of Year 5 decided to have some fun at Eric's expense on April Fool's day.

"Eh, Eric, over 'ere!" bellowed Peter, just before the bell for registration was due to ring.

"Are You Strong, Lass?"

"What's up? I can't mess about. I was late yesterday so am in trouble with Ma Watkins already," his squeaky-voiced victim replied.

"Message from old man Lane," continued Peter haughtily as an audience grew. "He needs yer to go to the science stores at morning break and ask Stuart for a couple o' things, a tin o' striped paint and while yer there, ask 'im if he can let yer 'ave a long stand."

The watching mob exchanged furtive, amused glances, knowing full well what game Salter was playing.

It was a crestfallen Eric Shepherd who was to be seen on the top corridor at the end of morning break after his futile and abortive mission to see Stuart, the science technician, who did not suffer fools gladly at the best of times.

The striped paint request had been met with the usual blank stare. This was, after all, a regular occurrence for Stuart but the long stand request had been successfully delivered.

Eric had been told to wait in the Prep room and he waited and waited and waited until Stuart informed him that he thought he had had a long enough stand.

Inevitably, the crowds had gathered on the top corridor and Eric heard 'April Fool' resound victoriously from every nook and cranny. He took it well because it was still preferable to being totally ignored as happened so often in his life.

MAY

Dear Mr and Mrs Waring,

As you are no doubt aware, the nurse was in school yesterday examining the children's heads for any outbreak of head lice. Your daughter, Julie, was unfortunately found to have quite a severe infestation and consequently it will be necessary for her to be treated with some solution designed to eradicate the problem as promptly as possible.

If you could make every effort to start the treatment as soon as possible, it would be very much appreciated; in the meantime if you could use a medicated shampoo like Wright's Coal Tar, that would help. Hopefully when she returns to school after the Whitsuntide break, it will no longer be a problem.

If you need any further guidance, we are able to put you in touch with the relevant authorities. My secretary will provide you with any information you may need. Thanking you for your understanding in this matter.

Yours sincerely,
J.T. Earl
Head of Year

THE weather in May tended to be pleasant, there was usually some degree of optimism in the air and quite a few enjoyable events in the school calendar to look forward to; trips abroad, days out on visits, lighter evenings and summer sports matches.

On the other hand, there were option choices to be made, parents' evenings and the dreaded French oral exams.

Long after school has become a distant memory for them, adults still recoil in horror whenever they recall a teacher eyeballing them, speaking largely incomprehensibly and nodding in their direction at regular intervals in some misguided attempt to make them answer an unfathomable question.

The topics had been prepared well in advance and concentrated on such areas as family, holidays, hobbies and school activities.

Sometimes an unseen reading passage was included as

well. But however well-prepared you were, the eight minutes in a tiny, stuffy cell-like room was a miniature version of hell.

In the background was the threatening and mechanical whirring of the two reel tape recorder as it recorded the responses for later grading.

Some of the kids just froze in fear and forgot everything that they had so meticulously revised for months, others coped well but did not realise that they had.

Some were determined that they would not do well and deemed the whole exercise a sorry shambles and complete and utter waste of their time.

It was very tiring, testing and quite stressful trying to ensure that you provided the optimum conditions for all your pupils and gave them the best opportunities to achieve their potential.

I enjoyed conducting the tests and I really wanted my protégées to do well. I used to get so disappointed if they missed a question or did not develop an answer to the full, especially if I knew that they had revised it thoroughly.

My French master, who was fondly remembered by successive generations of schoolchildren for his habit of throwing the very hard and unforgiving blackboard rubber in the direction of but never hitting inattentive pupils, was a wonderful, kind, modest and inspirational teacher.

He worked on a simple three word code, firm, fair and funny and all his lessons contained those elements.

Any success I may have achieved in my teaching career is largely attributable to him and following that notion. He became a family friend and played the organ at my wedding in 1970.

JUNE

Dear Miss,

We have to move house again. That man from the Council has been round. I can't really let on why but we have to so I am writing just to let you know so you can take our Kenneth off the register. He will be going to that new school on the other side of town near to the rugby ground.

It is a lot bigger and we think he will do OK. Your school has been alright but he is ready for a change like we all are.

Yours,

Mr and Mrs G. Lancaster

PS We think that you still owe us at least a week's dinner money.
PPS Do we need to give you the new address in case of anything that has to be sent on.
PPPS Just thought that you'll have to send the dinner money on anyway. So we will send you the new address as soon as possible. But would be obliged if you didn't let on to anyone where we are. We don't like people knowing our business.

WHITSUNTIDE was a glorious two week break but once back in the saddle, it was straight back to GCE 'O' Levels and internal examinations.

Intimidating rows of desks filled the entire assembly hall and it was a strange and frightening experience.

The hours went by very slowly from the command, "pick up your pens," and panic, regret and realisation set in alarmingly quickly among the pupils and helpless teacher invigilators whose frustrations at what they saw unfolding and the opportunities lost was, arguably, worse.

The biggest challenge for me was ensuring that I had written the correct period of elapsed time on the blackboard.

Working out what one and a quarter hours added onto 9.39am was could make me break out into a cold sweat, especially if I was being expected to field an array of off-putting questions at the same time.

On one occasion, a fight broke out and Darren Kendall broke John Holt's nose because he was sitting too near to his girlfriend Tracy Sparks, and getting a bit too familiar passing messages to her on scraps of paper.

Blood spilled everywhere and soaked the written offerings of both parties before any remedial action could be taken by a senior member of staff.

It led to much consternation in the staff room as to whether their answer sheets should be sent off to the examining body even if their overall mark wasn't likely to be affected or, indeed, what possible explanation could be given.

Evacuations from the hall during examinations were commonplace in my very early teaching days with the IRA increasing their mainland bombing campaigns.

It became commonplace for hoax telephone calls to be made to schools in order to cause disruption and draw attention to their political objectives.

Ours was no exception and such threats had to be taken seriously.

Neil Wright was a clever lad from a very humble background; he came from a big family and his father had died in a pit accident a few years previously.

He'd won a choral scholarship to the local cathedral and much of his time was taken up with choir practices and evensong.

He held his own admirably when he was initially teased by his chums and, because he was popular, very bright and a good sportsman, he was looked up to.

I discovered by chance when I was covering a lesson

for another colleague that he was equally proficient in English as he was in French.

He presented a speech which argued the case against keeping animals in zoos, in a mature and convincing manner and which had the class in rapt attention for the entire lesson.

I was so impressed with his performance that I took it upon myself to look into the possibility of entering him into a public speaking competition.

It would be new territory for me and even more so for the school. I confided in a few of my colleagues and received very mixed reactions which was understandable, I suppose.

Some of them clearly thought that I had delusions of grandeur, others that I was putting Neil and the school into an unfair situation and some that he deserved such an opportunity.

Having weighed up the pros and cons, I decided that I would go ahead with the idea and sought approval from the Headmaster who was enthusiastic despite his fears.

After giving me his blessing, I arranged to meet Neil for practice sessions during the dinner hour and between us we prepared a very creditable speech on the allotted topic of advertising.

I'll never forget walking into a huge and imposing room in Sheffield Town Hall on a warm June evening with him following close behind me, looking smart in his school uniform but at the same time, visibly apprehensive.

My husband and I had brought him, his sister and his mum with us in the car and they had gone on ahead while we completed the registration process.

In the public gallery, Mrs Wright was beaming from ear to ear, total and utter pride evident.

Her family didn't really get to do things like this; how his dad and his granddad would have loved this moment.

Neil did well and delivered his speech with a confidence way beyond his years.

He didn't win but was highly commended and we all knew that he had performed to the very best of his ability in a totally foreign world which was all that really mattered.

In later life, Neil went on to university and took up a responsible post in banking much to his mum's further delight.

JULY

Dear Mrs Padgett,

I just thought that I would write and let you know that Anne has finally completed her teacher training course at the college in Ripon.

As you know she went on to Sixth Form College to do her 'A' Levels in English Literature, French and History and she has really enjoyed all aspects of the training course. She decided eventually to specialise in main English with subsidiary games and she achieved a merit in the former and a commendation in the latter.

She had a fantastic time, did lots of travelling abroad and made some lovely new friends. She has really come out of her shell and gained a lot of confidence. We are so proud of her and feel that you, and lots of the other teachers at school, really inspired her and encouraged her to go further with her studies.

She is on holiday at the moment but I know that when she gets back she will want to come up to school to see you all. Hope this will be OK with everybody. She has got herself a job at a school in Leeds and is saving up for a second hand Ford Escort she has had her eye on for a while. But I'll let her tell you more about that herself.

Thank you again for all you did for her. It is much appreciated by me and her Dad.

Best wishes and thank you again. Have a wonderful holiday and a well-earned rest.

Shirley Miller

JULY was almost always a time of excitement and there seemed to be a permanent frisson of anticipation mingled in with the good weather as the school year hurried towards its end, the long lists of tasks to do before shutdown gradually being ticked off.

For some of the pupils, this was the end of school, a different world without all the rules and routines awaiting them; little did they know exactly what, as they prepared for assumed freedom.

For others it was a transition time as they prepared to go to other establishments to continue with their studies.

Varying but always honest reports were given out receiving mixed reactions but how many of them made it home, I'm not sure.

The final day of the summer term saw the very last school assembly for many and the build-up and lead in to it was interesting to say the least.

It was viewed by a caustic few as their last day before release from their own particular prison and the assumption was that the rules could be cast asunder and havoc wrought as and when they saw fit.

They came in modified uniform which often featured wearing their tie around the head, the wrong colour shirt or blouse and as much jewellery as they could find.

Large amounts of chocolate and sweets, gobstoppers and Bazooka Joe bubble gum would be eaten freely in class and even the more usually mild-mannered ones would challenge and argue with the staff about the most trivial issues.

"Are You Strong, Lass?"

I greatly admired the way in which the last day was handled by the teachers.

Meetings were held prior to the end of term where we were all briefed about the best way to handle this last and final onslaught. It was a finely-tuned procedure and more often than not it worked because there was understanding and tolerance in most cases.

Some of the more serious offenders were dealt with firmly and appropriately, but the mischievous activities were accepted as a rite of passage by the majority of staff as long as there was no threat to anyone else.

The antics included anything from locking the unwary in storerooms to tying underpants to a ruler and waving them out of an upstairs window.

Two boys once hijacked a milk float and arrived at school in style and some of the very toughest girls grabbed the poor, unsuspecting and very young woodwork master and kissed him repeatedly on the face and lips, leaving vivid imprints of Outdoor Girl Sexy Hot Pink lipstick plastered all over him.

By the time the bell tolled for that very last assembly, emotions and excitement were riding high.

The staff would march the classes in to the hall in as orderly and disciplined manner as was possible under the circumstances.

Potential troublemakers were isolated and made to sit under the very frightening and all powerful beady eye of the senior master.

More often than not, things went well and awards were presented to worthy recipients who proudly climbed the steps up to the stage to collect their trophies.

Hymns were belted out with great enthusiasm as their ending signalled the long break.

The end of the summer term often saw some of the teachers moving to pastures new as well or into deserved retirement.

Ceremonies and parties were arranged and the children presented their leaving gifts at the end of the assembly.

More often than not, they would also have undertaken a class collection and I never ceased to be genuinely moved and amazed at their generosity and goodwill on such occasions.

Even the rogues and vagabonds came good and would skulk awkwardly at the back of the classroom, muttering their best wishes while one of the pretty girls presented 'Sir' with his engraved Parker fountain pen or 'Miss' with a Wedgwood vase.

As soon as the kids had left, there was a bash in the staffroom with sausage rolls, cheese and pineapple on sticks, sandwiches, vol-au-vents and other buffet food spread out on a huge table.

Chairs were hastily re-arranged and the relieved gathered in groups to literally and metaphorically kick off their shoes.

The Headmaster would address the multitude about the year past and seek to embarrass those leaving when handing over more formal gifts of recognition.

There was a wonderful feeling of camaraderie and I loved such gatherings and remember them with great affection.

At one such, a well-respected and popular colleague was leaving to have a baby.

She was well-advanced into her pregnancy and had endured much good-natured teasing during the preceding months.

Some of the men staff thought it would be a good to

give her an appropriate send-off and to hoots of delight and shrieks of mild protestation, the poor lady was bundled, carefully but unceremoniously, into a large green Silver Cross pram and pushed out of the staffroom along the deserted corridors and back again.

The pram was decorated with balloons, ribbons and L Plates, with the lady's name on a poster flying high above it.

Another time, we presented among ourselves the 'Mushroom Awards' which had various sub divisions and categories.

Like the fungi, we all thrived and grew to our full potential as we were fed from on high with encouraging and wholesome information but which we at the time considered to be a load of manure.

We were also kept in the dark most of the time too.

Appropriate certificates had been designed by the art teacher and were presented in a mock ceremony amid thunderous applause and ribald laughter.

July also brought the jumble sale.

Redoubtable Miss D.M. Brooke, the deputy head, was heavily involved in the various planning stages as well as being the key figure on the day itself.

Any event in which she played a large part was guaranteed to be an occasion and never far from a witty remark.

As the many carrier bags of jumble cascaded into school on a regular basis in the lead up, her office began to resemble a rubbish tip.

Not wanting to discourage the pupils from their rare acts of magnanimity and selflessness, she would accept anything initially before holding an inquest at a later date to decide its fate and final destination.

Lamp standards, old transistor radios, crystal sets,

stuffed birds, snooker cues, plastic tablecloths, Playboy magazines, hearing aids, broken sunglasses, a toy donkey from Benidorm, an old bus conductor's cap and ticket machine, cake tins, artificial plants, flowers and somebody's grandma's ration book were placed in the 'white elephant' category at first and then attention was turned to the numerous clothes and shoes sent in.

In spite of the letter which had been sent out to parents advising them of the type of clothes which were desirable, and more importantly of those that were most definitely not, every imaginable item found its way into Miss Brooke's office.

Straw hats, rubber gloves, garters, scarves with "Love from Scarborough" embroidered on in loud and garish colours, chiffon blouses, bolero jackets, boiler suits, snake belts, bri-nylon nightdresses, crimplene jumpers, ladies' slacks, corsets (or roll-ons as Miss Brooke called them) knickers, string vests, underpants and socks full of holes were all deemed to be suitable for sale.

Why on earth would anyone think that is suitable for a school jumble sale?" she would utter with deep tones of despair in her voice as she picked her way through the various garments.

With teams of pupil helpers drafted in, she would oversee the great and grand sorting out process which largely involved tipping the majority into a huge dustbin and safeguarding the odd garment which she considered might just sell on a good day.

Huge piles would mount up in her office until very little else was visible.

Miss Brooke had selected the helpers carefully, employing her vast experience to flatter them and make them feel special.

They tended to be the ones who never really got chosen for anything and were almost social outcasts and who would put up with relentless teasing and taunting.

She would turn a blind eye to much of their bickering as to who should sort which pile as long as she possibly could but in the end would give both miscreants the benefit of one of her famous withering looks which immediately ended any dispute.

In the inner sanctum of her office instead of lessons, she generously dispensed squash and biscuits; Cadbury's chocolate fingers, Blue Ribands and Wagon Wheels were the height of luxury.

When the carrier bags were sorted and the argumentative skirmishes no more, the helpers were thanked graciously and ushered out of her office.

Some of them were quite reluctant to leave, there was not always much to go home to and they enjoyed being useful and valued.

Fortunately, that was not the end of their involvement.

When the day of the sale dawned, Miss Brooke would involve her team of helpers once more and she took immense pride from hearing the total raised when it was announced in assembly.

But it was more than the money.

AUGUST

Dear Mrs Padgett,

This is just a short note to thank you so much for all your help with Karen. We are really proud of what she has achieved while she has been in your class. We have seen her blossom from a mischievous tomboy into a confident young lady and we are really proud of her.

Neither me nor her Dad passed any of our exams at school so that makes it even more special for all the family.

She is hoping to go on to college and after that, who knows? Her granddad has told her that the world is at her feet if she works hard and that she will have opportunities that none of us ever did. We all know that she will make the best use of them and do us all proud.

Thank you again and please accept the enclosed Boots Voucher as a very small token of our appreciation. We hope you can buy something nice with it. Perhaps some perfume. Our Karen says that you like Aqua Manda by Goya and that you always smell nice. Enjoy the new term.

With best wishes,
Jean and Eric Saunders

EVERYONE breathed a sigh of relief and prepared to enjoy a modicum of relative peace and calm as August descended.

This was the time to take stock and any remedial building work undertaken at the school.

The corridors were now busy and bustling with very different people. Building contractors were drafted in to assess the extent of the work required and meetings set up to discuss the time scale and implications of the proposed schemes.

Workmen were scattered everywhere and would pop up in the most unlikely places carrying pieces of timber and various lengths of piping.

There were very few, if any, teachers in school on a regular basis and on the rare occasions I popped in, it always seemed an incongruous sight to see men in boiler suits carrying tool bags instead of uniform-clad boys and girls scurrying about their daily business.

There was an almost eerie feeling of desolation when

the children were not jostling and excitedly pushing their way from one place to another, even if it was easier to work on marking and administrative tasks without them around.

To me, the children were the life blood of the place and without their energetic and lively behaviour it merely resembled an empty shell.

The one August day the place resembled something like normality was when the exam results were posted.

It was usually the third Thursday of the month and the general office was the initial port of call and was the place where the dreaded outcomes were delivered.

Reactions varied; whoops of delight, shrieks of joy, gasps of relief, tears of happiness and disappointment.

Some of the teachers were stationed in their own classrooms and available for advice, mutual congratulations or a shoulder to cry on.

It was one of my very favourite days of the school year; all we had been working towards, a natural culmination of several years of very hard work and concentrated effort.

"Miss, Miss, I passed! Honest I did! Can't believe it! Is that fantastique or what?"

"I got the highest grade in French out of all my subjects! Amazing! All that hard work paid off! You said it would, didn't you, Miss?"

"Blimey, I did it. Don't know how but don't matter. And I did better than Foster!" All music to my ears.

Of course, it wasn't all good news. There were bitter pills for a few of them, some of which were predictable, others not. Whatever the outcome, I always tried to be on hand and offer advice regarding the next step.

One results day, I was aware that there was an advance party at my door, anxious to attract my attention before the general masses arrived.

It sadly transpired that Jeremy Pollard's father had passed away the previous evening quite unexpectedly from a massive heart attack at the age only forty-one.

Jeremy was one of my high achieving pupils who had a very promising future ahead of him and I was extremely fond of him and his elder brother who I had taught as well.

His friends told me that he desperately wanted to come into school to collect his results even though he could scarcely grasp the awful reality of his situation.

I can see his face now as vividly as if it was only yesterday, his face pale and eyes dark and raw.

And yet, he had a strange glow about him which suggested a pride in his achievements in spite of his tragic loss because he had gained the highest possible grade in all of his nine subjects.

In his typically modest way he looked me full in the face and somehow found some words.

"Thank you for all your help and support, Miss. I couldn't have done it without you. My mum will be chuffed to bits."

I smiled at him and assured him that his results were attributable to his hard work and ability rather than to anything that I had done.

He nodded graciously and as he moved towards the classroom door, flanked by his loyal and supportive friends, he turned towards me and added, "My dad will be pleased as well won't he?"

Post academia, he went on to enjoy a very successful and rewarding career with a finance company but he'd graduated with honours in character long before that.

10.

Yorkshire Relish

Dear Miss,

It's all about our Melanie's ears. Her Granny and Gramps decided to spend a bit of money on her for her 14th birthday last month. They normally just buy her a record or a bit of make up but because her Gramps had had a bit of luck on the dogs at the Doncaster track they decided to spoil her a bit.

So, they asked her what she would like and she said was to have her ears pierced and some gold sleepers fitted. But now she tells me that you've asked her to take them out because it's against the school rules.

I know that you have to have rules but I don't see how our Melanie wearing some earrings is going to cause a lot of trouble or bother. She can't take them out though because her ear holes will heal up and she will have to have them done again and we can't afford it.

I do hope you can sort it out and have a word with the headmaster and help him to change his mind.

Yours faithfully,
Mrs Lesley Stevenson (Mother)

"EH up, Miss, I think you used to teach me!"

I lost track of the times that I bumped into former pupils who I'd help set on their way, even in those early, formative teaching years and, in so many ways, that was the greatest source of gratification.

On hearing their greeting, I was right back there with them whether it was in the classroom, on the games field or a coach to France.

It is true that I remembered some more fondly than others but I was always extremely gratified that they wanted to talk to me and had some wonderful and emotional conversations with some of them sharing the details of our respective lives.

I'd been admitted to hospital for the imminent arrival of my first baby and had settled myself as comfortably as I could in readiness for the midwife's examination when I heard. "Well, if it's who I think it is, I am sure you used to teach me at secondary school."

A pretty and petite young nurse emerged into the delivery room and I realised, despite the gas and air, that it was Catherine Wilkinson who had been in my first GCE 'O' Level French class.

She had been one of my very best girls, a hard worker who was determined to succeed and a pleasant and reliable character as well.

I have never forgotten how kind, considerate and professional she was. My baby was a little reluctant to make his way into the world and she changed her shift with another midwife so that she could stay with me until the appointed time.

It was a strange sense of role reversal.

IN time, I had numerous drinks bought for me, shoes repaired for free, reduced price concert tickets and restaurant and hotel reservations for which I am incredibly grateful.

I've come across former pupils in all walks of life. Gas Board employees and electricians have responded to my requests for home visits, I've been greeted at supermarket checkouts, looked after by receptionists at the doctors and had details of my will transcribed by a legal secretary.

They were very proud, and justifiably so, of their achievements in the world of work, and were eager to show me how well they had done.

I was delighted to share their success; it was part justification of trying to give them a start in life.

Often, I would come across them in town on a Saturday with their own children in tow and glowing with pride to show off their offspring.

It never ceased to amaze me that, long after they had been forced to sit in my classroom and listen to me drone on about something they were not really interested in, they still addressed me as Miss.

During a spell of severe wintry weather a few years ago, I found myself stranded on a train for three hours when we juddered to an undignified halt half a mile from our destination.

We were well and truly stuck so I settled down and tried to make the best of it.

Directly opposite was a lady totally engrossed in the intricacies of her mobile phone.

I hadn't really taken much notice of her but as we both

looked up simultaneously, she said, "Hi there Miss. 'Ow are you doing? Thought it was you on the platform when we got on back in Wakey."

I looked to see Marilyn Darwin of Form E3 who had always been pouting and flirting, and tossing her hair back provocatively, a fourteen-year-old bane of my classroom endeavours.

Time had not been kind to her and she looked much older than her years. Decades of hard living, too many Park Drive and a general unhealthy life style had taken its toll on her.

"Well, hello there Marilyn. I can see who it is now. How are you? What are you up to these days?" I asked rather tentatively.

She told me that she was working in a city centre sports shop as an assistant manager and helping out at another one when she was able.

We chatted for a while, remembering various incidents and laughing about them now, whereas I and other staff had near-wept about them at the time.

I was pleased that she felt confident and able to make herself known to me and that she was doing something positive with her life.

She showed me photos of her children and partner and shared her hopes for the future with me.

Our conversation over, her mobile phone rang and the last words I heard as she went to stretch her legs, were, "Eh, Guess what? I've been stuck on this bloody train for about two hours wi' mi' old French teacher! Yer remember her, don't yer? Course yer do! She don't seem as bad as I thought she were."

Angela was the daughter of a local jeweller who had his shop in town and ran quite a thriving business.

It was a long-established family firm, she was very proud of it and earned a little pocket money by working there in the school holidays and at weekends.

She was a pretty girl and was a big hit with all the customers and her time there also allowed her to dream.

Academically, she was below average and perhaps destined to join the ranks of the vast army of unskilled workers but she was desperate to become a model and spend her life on catwalks, in magazines and travelling the world.

I couldn't blame her; if such kids were deprived of their ability to see a way out, then they would really would have very little reason to get out of bed on a morning.

Angela would select her make up for school carefully, making very good use of her Miners block mascara which she had to spit on so that the little brush would glide smoothly.

She would always make the very best of her navy blue gymslip by hitching it up as far as she dared, white blouse and very plain black shoes in order to create the most fashionable look of the time.

She paraded around the corridors and told anyone who would listen about her hopes for the future.

She had plans. She had no intention whatsoever of staying around 'in this dump,' she was going places.

It was never quite clear to anyone where exactly she was going or how she intended to get there and achieve such ambitions.

To this day, every time I go shopping in one of the larger department stores in town, I try to visit the cafe and restaurant; I know that Angela will be there, like she has been for the last seventeen years.

Her teenage dream, predictably and sadly, amounted to nothing and she has been clearing tables and serving coffee and cakes in a collection of establishments since she left school.

And she has been doing a very good job as well – she is a much-respected and valued member of staff.

I always catch her eye and we enjoy a good chat and a trip down memory lane. In my mind's eye, I can still see that young girl with all her fanciful aspirations and I hope that she still possesses both the strength and inclination to dream big whenever she can.

I bumped into Sandra quite recently.

Initially I didn't recognise her but as she approached me to ask the time, my memory kicked in, "Why it's Sandra Marshall, isn't it?" I said, remembering the shy and rather awkward lass who had struggled with several aspects of her schooling and relationships with her peer group.

"Yeah, it is. Fancy you knowing me after all these years," she responded quietly.

We chatted for a short while. She filled me in on the numerous jobs she'd had since leaving school and seemed reasonably satisfied with her lot.

Suddenly, without warning, and within the space of about thirty seconds, she recounted the desperately sad chain of events which had dogged her young life.

She had lost her husband to cancer at a very early age, her toddler son had been killed in a road accident and her mum and dad had disowned her because they did not like her new boyfriend.

It was delivered in a matter of fact manner and she wasn't looking for sympathy, just someone she trusted to unburden on.

I managed to offer her some words of comfort before she suddenly realised that she was late for work, detached herself, shouted a hasty farewell and disappeared.

"Are You Strong, Lass?"

Dear Mr Yates,

I am writing to you on behalf of the whole teaching staff to offer you and your family our most sincere sympathy on the recent and most untimely death of your wife. The school has been aware of the very difficult family circumstances which you have had to shoulder over the last few months and we have tried to be as understanding as possible.

We will do our very best as a school to support you, Marie and Paul in any way we can. I know that it will be a difficult time for you all but I am sure that if we work positively together then we can make the best out of a very sad situation. The children's respective class teachers will be in touch with you before too long to discuss the best way forward for everyone.

Once again, please be assured of our deepest sympathy, and do not hesitate to get in touch with the school if there is anything at all as can do.

Yours sincerely,
Mr Stanley Cowburn
Headmaster

11.

Yorkshire Puddings

Dear Mr and Mrs Clapham,

I am writing to inform you that, as from the beginning of next term, your son, Shaun, and daughter, Melanie, will be entitled to free school meals, due to a change in circumstances at Mr Clapham's workplace and a reduction in his working hours.

You do not need to do anything and both your children's names will be added to the free school meals register. If there is any further information you require then please do not hesitate to contact school.

Yours sincerely
Mr Stanley Cowburn
Headmaster

WHEN I began teaching in 1970, about sixty-eight percent of pupils had school dinners and the cost per meal was one shilling and sixpence. Shortly afterwards, the government announced its intention to increase the price and they rose to almost double.

I have largely fond memories of taking the dinner register. Columns and rows would dance before my eyes every Monday morning as I tried in vain to attract attention and get the pupils to commit to the notion that they might just be staying for dinner that day.

"Steven Lane, are you staying or not? Simple enough question, isn't it? Bring your money out right now please."

"Steven Lane! Did you hear me? Put that Hotspur comic down right now, for goodness sake. We haven't got all day, you know".

"Aw Miss it's not that easy. Our old bid 'as only given mi enough for three days but I 'ave to stay for four cos she's going away to visit mi Nan in Brid and, I 'ad to gi' our Kevin some brass this morning for him to give to Fat Baz or else he's gonna bray him after school."

Such a scenario was a regular part of the Monday morning routine.

Miraculously, the register did get completed and, more often than not, the money added up correctly and was sent to the office with it, the neat black and the vivid red biro absence circles inserted in the correct place and the free school dinners column filled in.

For some pupils, dinners was the highlight of the day – it provided a social opportunity as well as a hot meal that was something in short supply for a majority.

There was just a chance that, with the hastening onset of puberty, they might get to make eye contact and exchange sly smiles with someone they fancied in another class and didn't get to see on a regular basis.

Or get somebody else to surreptitiously pass a message,

written on a scruffy bit of exercise book paper, to the object of their heart's desire.

I intercepted many such romantic missives in my early days and must confess that I found them great fun and optimistically encouraging provided there was no lewd content.

If there was, I'd blush and pass the notes on promptly to my superiors to deal with.

There wasn't as much mixing of the sexes, pupils were separated during the school day on a regular basis and so they had to take their chances when and where they could.

The meal itself, though so often the subject of fun, was a life line to many growing up in tough circumstances, it was a safety net; green custard and all.

The vast majority of families were very appreciative and eternally grateful.

In my first post, the dining room was the area that greeted you as you approached the school from down the drive with a huge chimney-like structure that housed a boiler and extractor catching the attention and assailing the senses.

From the moment of arrival the smells of cooking assailed, capable of being both off-putting and appetising as the morning wore on.

The way into the dining room was through sliding partition doors which opened onto quite a small and thereby intimate area which was expected to feed a large number of staff and pupils.

A serving hatch at the far end was manned by about four or five dinner ladies who ruled with a rod of iron.

Not to be messed with, there was no arguing, no answering back, no negotiating, no changing your mind; it was no manners, no dinner.

In what was known as 'family service,' the dinners

were served at each table by the older pupils who collected the courses from the hatch in tureens and carried it back rather precariously.

As the food was distributed, requests would fly across the dining room.

"I don't want none of that horrible cabbage stuff and give me a small potato," one lad would shout.

"Small sponge and none of that custard, please," a little girl's voice would utter, bravely.

On some occasions the staff would sit with the children and participate; on others we might be on duty and be required to keep a watchful eye on proceedings but, in general, there was a unity of purpose.

The dinner ladies knew the kids inside out and would look out for them and encourage them to eat and build up their strength.

They were in turn respected by the pupils who appreciated their concern and motherly approach.

The dinner ladies could get through to them in a very different way than us teachers and often acted as a go between in difficult and sensitive circumstances.

They were very good cooks too but the basic, generally unimaginative ingredients and facilities with which they had to work did not always allow them to do justice to their skills.

Among the less popular dishes were brisket, round slices of cold beef interlaced with more white fat and gristle than meat, steamed fish, which was always served as a lumpy mass and appeared to be grey in colour.

Everyone knew from very early on in the day when that item was on the menu because the smell permeated the entire bottom corridor and the adjacent assembly hall, lingering the whole day long.

It came with lumpy and gelatinous parsley sauce.

Then there was Kit-e-Kat pie, so-called because the sardine and tuna mix on top of the hard pastry case greatly resembled the look of cat food despite the addition of random, luminous green processed peas which were scattered on top in an attempt to improve its look.

Swede was a regular and hated vegetable which was often served lumpy and soggy, and at the end of each sitting it was present, mountains of it could be seen in the slops bucket despite regular lectures from the starched-uniformed dinner ladies about the immorality of waste.

One of the big favourites was Manchester Tart, which was a very popular dessert with strawberry jam and set custard on a crisp pastry base, topped with banana and sometimes desiccated coconut. Gooseberry crumble was the most popular dessert, apple pie a great favourite with custard, along with meat and potato pie with its rich and thick gravy and light delicious pastry.

There was also semolina with red jam mixed in to make it turn pink, rice pudding, jam roly-poly and treacle, ginger or currant sponge, all of them an ideal end to a meal on a cold winter's day, especially after stew and dumplings.

Calories tended to disappear running around the playground for the rest of the dinner hour, often to keep warm and there were no snacks available between meals.

Before eating there was always the cursory grace said by a member of staff, "For what we are about to receive, may the Lord make us truly thankful," during which everyone bowed their heads and mumbled along with the words.

Once, when we were celebrating all things Yorkshire, one of the older, male teachers came up with, "God bless us all an' mak us able, ta eyt all t'stuff 'at's on this table," which caused much amusement.

Drink to accompany was tap water from a brightly-coloured metallic jug into small tumblers whose manufacturer's name, Duralex, caused much innuendo and many a smutty comment from growing adolescents.

Once the meals were over and the plates sided off, then the older pupil in nominal charge of the table organised the final part of the family service contract, setting.

Everybody hated it but all the tables had to be grudgingly re-laid with crockery, cutlery, glasses and jugs under the watchful eye of the poor unfortunate teacher who happened to be on duty, in readiness for the next onslaught.

Dear Miss,

I am sorry that Jamie has not been in school for the last few days but he has been poorly with a right bad belly ache. It turned out to be an upset stomach and a right bad case of dire-rear. We reckon it might ave been that pie he had for his school dinner yesterday. He seems a bit better now so I have sent him to school today. Keep an eye on him if you would because it won't be a pretty sight if it all kicks off again, believe me.

Thank you,
Mrs Mary Bowers.
PS. He has some pink stuff in a bottle in his school bag if you could make sure he takes some please. He also has some spare underpants. Just in case.

12.

Yorkshire Folk

Dear Miss,

Do I need an appointment to see the headmaster or not? Some folk think I do but the woman next door reckons I don't. Perhaps you can tell me but don't let on to our Brian that I have written cos he'll go mental.

Anyway, I'd like to come and talk about his behaviour. Since his dad died I have found it really hard to keep him in line and his sisters are a bit of a handful as well. I just want Mr Cowburn to know that he can do what he likes with him.

I'm not one of these mams who will be rushing up to school to complain every five minutes. If he needs a good crack or a slippering, then you have my full permission.

I do try my best, honest I do, but he lacks a bloke's influence and I don't want him getting out of control. After all, he is only 13 and there's a long way to go yet.

"Are You Strong, Lass?"

I would be grateful if you could let me know what's what and then we can get something sorted.

Thank you,
Lynda Williams

THE majority of parents were a truly amazing bunch of people; gritty, down to earth and what you saw was what you got. They spoke their mind whether it was appropriate or not.

A good number of them were very fair and open to advice but, unfortunately, there was always a small group who could be confrontational, loud, opinionated and misguided.

Some of them even liked a fight. Why use words when a good smack across the face did the job in half the time – and that was as much from women who carried a sense of injustice for their children.

Up to school they'd march on receipt of a letter about the behaviour of their precious ones, or on hearing innuendo, often accompanied by a dog the size of a pony with an endearing name like Satan or Fang.

They would march purposefully and defiantly down the school drive, their emotions and feelings written on their face and warning others not to get in their way.

Matters were usually sorted out amicably after initial misunderstandings were explained and expletives released and often a determining factor underlying the confrontations was the amount of alcohol consumed by the accuser prior to the visit.

I remember vividly one of the parents, Mr Fielding, staggering down the drive with one hand attached to the lead of a massive, evil-looking dog and the other clutching a bottle of Newcastle Brown proclaiming in no uncertain terms what he was going to do to that bloody headmaster.

He had to be steered through the main door by the senior master and manoeuvred into the office as quickly as possible before a large group assembled in the entrance hall and cheered him on.

As a young teacher, I was always impressed that parents who behaved like this were allowed in and not immediately shoved back out.

There always seemed to be a genuine desire to work things out in everyone's best interests, however futile it might have appeared.

In a peculiar sort of way, Mr Fielding and the other parents like him were only trying to do the best for their children and it was the only method they knew.

Many endured very hard and deprived lives with little material or emotional comfort and were confused and, I daresay, frightened at the thought of dealing with their teenage offspring and meeting teachers.

In the majority of cases we did help them to sort out those problems, even if it was only a temporary fix.

Nevertheless, overall there was more acceptance of the school's authority and the decisions made and a large number came to compliment the Headmaster on the way he had handled certain sensitive issues or to offer their services to the Parent Teacher Association.

Parents' evenings were always interesting and frequently eventful.

For some, coming up to school was a rare chance to strut their stuff, to be part of a big show and an opportunity to be the centre of attention and make an impression – we could see where their kids got it from.

Mrs Naylor came complete in her plastic pink hair rollers and slightly shabby apron and ended up following a young and desperately reluctant biology teacher down the corridor, him protesting in an increasingly rising voice that he did not think it would be a good idea to go back to her place so they could discuss 'her Terry' in more comfortable surroundings.

He was a lovely chap, very popular with staff and pupils alike and well-read in his subject. Not long out of university, he was not yet comfortable in this harsher, northern real world and was of a very trusting and gullible nature.

Double-entendres were lost on him and it took him a long time to realise that Mrs Naylor's interpretation of the biology syllabus was not quite the same as his.

He was inevitably the butt of much good-natured teasing in the staffroom for many a month afterwards.

Inevitably, though, those parents who you desperately needed to talk to about misbehaviour and lack of progress with their kids, were rarely in evidence, which again told its own story.

As a staff, we really did try hard to accommodate the parents and their lifestyles. Occasionally, we rearranged times and dates so that some of them could still go to darts night at their local pub, catch the last bingo session at the Mecca in town or take part in the snooker finals at the working men's club.

Even though I was a young, inexperienced teacher who very quickly realised that graduate teacher status did not seem to count for much at all, I tried really hard to empathise with parents.

It must have been a huge ordeal for some of them to hold a meaningful conversation with certain members of the staff in particular, especially dads who appeared to find it harder to talk in those formal surroundings.

They felt inferior and intimidated by the academic

setting they had often struggled with, and believed that they couldn't really hold their own in any verbal exchange.

Often it was not true but they did not possess the confidence to dare to change such preconceptions.

Regrettably, a small minority of the teachers enjoyed making them feel small and adopted a supercilious and high-handed attitude to emphasise their learnedness.

I remember feeling very annoyed when I came across or heard about it and thought it most unfair although I dare not say anything at the time.

A few parents were articulate and knowledgeable, came well prepared and were very keen to share their opinions about their young one's prospects although back then it wasn't really an interactive process with the subjects present.

They were, more likely, waiting fearfully at home for news.

I always enjoyed parents' evening and never saw it as the kind of bind some older colleagues did and resented.

Meeting the parents and comparing notes helped me to understand and influence their children positively.

It was so important to connect and engage meaningfully with them so that everyone could work together in order to give the children the best possible options, especially in a tough inner city school.

And it was particularly heart-warming to observe their obvious pride when they were told how well theirs was doing.

A lot of the parents I encountered in those early days had not followed, and so struggled to understand an examination course.

That wasn't because they weren't clever enough but various social and financial reasons had taken precedence.

Almost all were genuinely delighted that the next generation did not have such obstacles in their way and that their prospects appeared better.

Dear Miss Padgett,

Just to let you know that both Kevin's dad and me will be coming to Parents Evening on Thursday 23rd March. I expect that you will be very surprised given our track record of late. However, it is not quite as straightforward as it might seem.

On no account do I want to bump into his dad at the meeting. As you know we have been divorced for a good year now and he doesn't normally concern himself with things at school. This Parents Evening is different for him though, because he wants to make sure that Kevin chooses his 'O' Level and CSE subjects carefully and sensibly.

He doesn't think that I am capable of stating my opinions strongly enough, fighting Kevin's cause or guiding him to make the best possible choices. I only went to a secondary modern school, after all, as he reminds me at every available opportunity.

So would it be possible for you to see us separately at different times, please? I do not think I could trust myself to behave if I had to sit next to him for ten minutes. I appreciate that it might need a bit of planning but I would be really grateful, it could save us all from a very embarrassing incident.

Thanking you in advance for your cooperation in this matter. Please don't hesitate to get in touch before the meeting if you need to. I would not want anything to go amiss for everybody's sake.

Yours sincerely,
Karen Armitage (MRS) (unfortunately)

13.

A Right Yorkshire Mixture

Dear Miss,

Please will you thank the headmaster for his letter which we got last Thursday telling us about our Trevor wagging off school. Both me and his dad have had a right good chat about it and we thought we'd rather write to you than to the headmaster if that's OK. You can then pass it on if you see fit.

After talking to our Trevor, we have found out that he just gets bored in lots of lessons and would rather be helping his cousin on the market stall. He gets a bit of money as well and he really enjoys it. We have told him he hasn't to do it and that he only has another few weeks to do at school and then he can leave for good.

He has listened but we are not sure if we really got through to him or not. His idea of listening and mine are not the same.

He did make quite a good point though. He said that he goes to school, gets there on time and gets his mark in the register and then wags off on his way to the first lesson. He reckons that if he gets to school, then it's your job to make sure he stays there.

Can you have a word with somebody and get back to us please as soon as possible. We do need to get it sorted out as quickly as we can.

Yours,
Freda Spillane

I ATTENDED staff meetings at my teaching practice school although, in truth, I never paid much attention in them, I'm ashamed to admit.

I was required to sit in as part of my qualification process but never really felt involved because I suppose I didn't actually belong there nor understand or grasp the processes and importance. But my first proper staff meeting in the very first term of my initial real job was certainly an eye opener, on a stuffy and humid late afternoon in June.

With the kids long gone to pursue their paper rounds, babysitting duties, swimming down the quarry or anything other than their homework, the staff hastily downed a reviving cup of tea and the men dragged the chairs in the staffroom into some sort of circle and awaited the arrival of the headmaster who was to chair the meeting.

It wasn't a very big area, a rectangular-shaped refuge badly in need of redecoration and with seats that were upholstered in a mix of different fabrics.

There were some prints in old fashioned frames hung precariously on the walls, one in particular of a clown particularly disconcerting as I always felt its piercing stare was directed at me.

It transpired that the only criteria for display was not aesthetic but if the pictures were cheap and fit in the back of rural studies teacher, Mr Johnson's old van.

Eventually the meeting staggered to a somewhat hesitant start, the headmaster himself late and then followed in by the remedial studies and biology teachers who had been further delayed by the minutiae of their day.

The meeting was conducted in a much more informal way than I'd imagined. Eventually it came to order and the head started by welcoming Vernon and myself to the school and said some extremely complimentary things about what he anticipated we'd bring to it; I blushed and Vernon shuffled uncomfortably.

All of a sudden, there was an almighty bang and a loud clanking sound which made me jump and shattered the relative calm.

Casting my eyes in the direction of the brouhaha at the far end, I was astonished to see a large metal bucket gripped by yellow marigolds swing its way into the room, closely followed by a rather stout lady with curly ginger hair and a very red face.

"Oh my Gawd, so sorry Headmaster! I really didn't know you 'ad a meeting on tonight. Well, if I did I'd gone and forgotten. Don't usually 'ave 'em on a Monday do yer? You see I wanted to get finished so that I can meet our Angela and see what the doc 'as to say about 'er infection," said the bucket's owner, Mrs Venables as Stanley Cowburn politely shooed her away.

She retreated, backing out the way she came saying something about coming back tomorrow to finish up.

No one else flinched at what, apparently was, a regular occurrence.

The rough agenda – more a batting order – looked pretty dull; the store room door locks, when the caretaker should take his lunch break and the escalating cost of postage among the items for discussion.

The staff shuffled about, got up to make cups of tea and popped out to the toilet whenever they felt like it. Andy Fellows from biology smoked his way through a whole packet of Embassy, coughing at the most inappropriate times and Laura Keen who was a supply teacher at the time, fell asleep during the discussion about exam invigilation.

We talked about the pupils and their problems, solving some and leaving others for a later date, planned the order of events for sports day which was to be held later in the term and addressed the thorny problem of putting the children in the correct option groups for the new term.

It caused some lively debate not least because the school was gradually evolving from what had been a secondary modern in part to a fully-fledged comprehensive, and priorities were naturally changing.

One lad of ability became a tug of war between the respective teachers of religious studies, rural studies and history, each feeling that he would be better suited to their sphere of influence where he would be likely to get better marks that would reflect well on the school.

I suddenly realised that such meetings to determine whether the level of academic or practical prowess were likely to be more productive for both pupil and establishment had particular significance.

In the end Mrs Norris, an affable, ruddy complexioned middle-aged woman who had made Vernon and I so welcome from the off, won the day, defeated Jonno who was making his excuses and leaving as Dusty Miller beside him mouthed, 'darts match' to anyone looking his way.

There were no official minutes taken although the school secretary popped in occasionally and any notes relating were pinned up on the staffroom notice board the following day to inform and remind what had gone on.

If multiple copies were required they were produced on the Banda with its foul-smelling coloured ink before that was superseded by Roneo which spat out duplicates as you turned a handle forcefully for what seemed like an eternity.

In spite of such basic communications, we were largely aware of what was going on and the senior staff in particular had their finger on the pulse.

At that first meeting we also talked a lot about a family experiencing several emotional problems, and it was agreed to support a boy in the fourth form who was trying to raise money to help his disabled brother by holding a jumble sale one evening after school.

A list was circulated which contained the names of pupils who were going to be recommended for a place on the Direct Grant Scheme, their parents to be invited into school to discuss the options and way forward in what would be a big step into new territory.

Around the same time, I was introduced to written reports detailing the pupil's progress which were sent out twice a year.

They were extremely basic – a single line entry per subject coupled with a cursory mention of any clubs and societies to which they belonged, how many times they'd been absent and a paragraph at the bottom for the form teacher's comments.

Parents were not even required to countersign that they had received, never mind read it.

All the report sheets had to remain in the staffroom so that the recalcitrant could be chivvied along to complete their section – not that the edict stopped some from spiriting them away in their briefcases to complete in the relative quiet and comfort of their own home.

A large table was cleared of its customary junk and

coffee cups and the reports laid out in form order, making it easier for us to pick out the relevant piles.

On occasions, mark books could be seen as a memory aid but, more often than not, a lot of it was done without reference to anything apart from a teacher's insight and judgement.

Ashtrays were positioned at strategic points for those who had a fag roll around the side of their mouths as they wrote, the exercise dominating free periods or before and after the school day as the deadlines loomed.

Whenever we were in session, there were a stream of questions, many hypothetical, tossed into the on-going conversation.

"How do you spell conscientious?"

"Just put hardworking."

"I don't know what to say about Steven Porter, I find him a real enigma. Sometimes he can produce excellent and thought-provoking work and often he writes the biggest load of twaddle that you could ever imagine."

"What's the name of that fat lad in my third year lower set? I can never remember, I always want to call him 'Clearasil', mother's a greyhound trainer. Their faces all merge after a while."

We were also expected to fit in an effort and achievement grade alongside, usually based on combining the marks from a couple of last minute one-off tests, no matter how unfair that seemed to those who had done well on a weekly basis.

Some of the comments were near the knuckle. Steve Green, who taught English just entered, "Who? I've not clapped eyes on him since Christmas" on Leslie Street's report with a quick flourish of his chewed black biro.

The lad was barely there because of some extenuating

circumstances, but Steve wanted to make the point that he could hardly be expected to teach and grade someone who was rarely around.

Steve's other stock remark which he would reproduce at regular intervals was, "No pen. No pencil. No book. No progress. No point."

The geography teacher, George Porter, insisted he crafted every word in fountain pen ink and dabbed carefully with pink blotting paper to ensure that the next author would not smudge his best hand.

Invariably, in just one line, a half year's work was succinctly, expertly and often wittily summed up and that was a gift.

Malcolm Denham was in charge of physics. He was a very good teacher and he also put in a lot of extra time helping to coach the school swimming teams.

His memory was not as sharp as it could have been but his commitment and swimming knowledge could not be faulted and he clearly cared for his flock.

The star of the under 14s boys' squad was a lad called Anthony Whitehead, who was also a twin although not an identical one. His brother Timothy was also a lovely lad but he could not manage a breadth of the baths.

The irate phone call which was put through to the staffroom the day after the reports were sent home became legend.

Mrs Whitehead was not a lady to be messed with. Her boys were her life since Mr Whitehead had moved out of the family home when the twins were six years old to live with Sharon the local hairdresser. But she had an unfortunate way of expressing herself; she meant well but her flaring temper tended to get in the way.

"I really don't know where or how to begin, Mr

Denham. You cannot imagine, even in your wildest dreams, how very angry I am!" she said when telephoning in to speak to the teacher.

"Hello Mrs Whitehead. I was going to ring you as soon as I got a minute? Your Anthony will need to bring that deposit in pretty sharpish if he wants to be included in the inter-school swimming gala next week."

That merely stoked her ire. "Well that just takes the biscuit, it really does! Do you have any idea what the purpose of this telephone call is or are you completely stupid and insensitive?" she regaled.

Taken aback somewhat, Malcolm replied, "Now, now come on, Mrs Whitehead. There's no need to take on so. I only asked for the deposit and it is a week late at least."

"You really do have no idea, do you? My son is the star of your swimming team and you can't even get his damn name correct on his report. It's disgraceful. You didn't even put his twin brother's name! Just some random one like Brian. There isn't even a Brian in the team as far as I am aware."

The contrite teacher merely compounded his error by saying, "Oh, right, I see, that's why you rang me, I was wondering. If you send his report back in the morning, I'll put it right and change it to Brian, we all know who we mean. And don't forget that deposit."

At which point the phone was slammed down at the other end.

Dear Mr and Mrs Lawson,

I am writing to you about Lee's attitude to Miss Barclay, the biology teacher.

She has had a lot of trouble with him in class recently and has asked me to contact you as a last resort after several attempts to resolve the situation.

During a recent lesson, he would not sit down in his seat and persisted in shouting and showing off throughout the entire session. The topic for discussion was, 'The life cycle and reproductive habits of the common toad.'

Lee delighted in yelling out obscenities and asking highly inappropriate questions. When she tried to remonstrate with him, he became abusive and even more awkward. As his Head of Year I feel compelled to share this incident of bad behaviour with you especially after the discussion we had following the receipt of his school report.

As you are aware, Lee is a clever boy with good prospects and we must put a stop to this unacceptable behaviour immediately. He must realise before it is too late that playing class clown is in nobody's interests.

I trust that I have your full support in this matter and I would be grateful if you could contact the school to arrange a mutually convenient time for us to meet and discuss the matter further.

Yours sincerely,
David Bourne,
Head of Year Three

14.

Yorkshire Tykes

Dear Mrs Padgett,

I am writing this letter in order to ask your permission for something important. My son, Riaz, has been invited to attend the local Mosque for two days next week in order to take part in a special service to celebrate the feast of Ramadan. He will be reading from the Koran and reciting prayers.

As you are no doubt aware, this is a very important feast for Muslim families and we feel very honoured and privileged that he has been selected as one of the main participants.

I do hope that you will be able to grant permission and that you will help Riaz catch up on any school work which he will miss. We do not want him to fall behind with his studies. We value his education opportunities very much and like to think we encourage him all we can. Thank you very much indeed.

Bibi Mohammed [Mrs]

AS well as a good mixture of abilities, types and characters, we also attracted a number of different ethnic backgrounds to the school in those early days in the 1970s.

There were Asian pupils, West Africans and several children from Eastern Europe, notably Yugoslavians and Poles.

I don't remember any trouble or racial conflict at all in spite of the varied mix.

The pupils rubbed along well together in the main; what mattered to them was whether their classmates were fair and reliable, how skilled they were in athletics, swimming or football and whether they shared a wicked sense of humour.

The school was in the middle of a large estate which had forged strong links with mining stretching back years.

The families from Eastern Europe had come to England to seek employment in the coal industry and we were very fortunate to have their children in our charge.

Nearly all of them had an admirable work ethic and were keen to learn and take advantage of the educational opportunities on offer to them.

They fitted in well and played a full and willing part in the life of the school, often excelling in both academic work and sporting activities of all kinds.

Their parents were very modest and proud people who had endured much hardship and were extremely grateful that their children had been given the chance to improve their long term career prospects.

I used to love talking to them at parents' evenings and sharing in their undoubted pride when they were told of their children's achievements.

The vast majority were always supportive and anxious

to help in any way they could. Some of their kids went on to become G.P.s or worked in dentistry or ophthalmology.

Others became engineers and architects, musicians and teachers also with reliability and conscientiousness at their core.

One or two, though, did have their problems and demons.

Grigori, in particular, really struggled for a variety of reasons. He was tall and physically strong, popular within his peer group and he excelled at sport.

Inside the classroom he was always more comfortable with mathematically based subjects in which he was quite proficient.

However, put him into a situation where he had to perform any sort of language-based tasks and his self-esteem plummeted.

Not because English wasn't his first language but it appeared rather to stem from a basic inability to order his thoughts into any sort of pattern.

He would become obstructive and violent, swearing and lashing out at anyone who tried to restrain him.

It was as if his brain seemed to overload and then close down and once becalmed, usually by the senior master who had been summoned for support, he would adopt a womb-like position and curl up on his seat and rock backwards and forwards with his thumb in his mouth.

It was a difficult situation for all concerned, I found him hard to deal with and was frightened of his outbursts but I did share his frustrations.

He was a clever lad and it didn't make any sense at all although with the advantage of hindsight, I have come to realise that he was probably dyslexic, not something we could identify then.

The children of Asian background also contributed much to all aspects of school life.

Their parents and relatives had principally come to the United Kingdom in the 1950s to search for work in the mills and factories.

They had established small communities, worked extremely hard to establish themselves and had just become noticeable as owners of corner shop convenience stores.

In the main, the children settled in well. The girls did not enjoy as much freedom as the boys which caused some consternation but seemed to be accepted practice.

Parents, especially fathers, sometimes had to be reminded that their daughters were just as clever as their sons, and in some cases, brighter.

They had grand ambitions for their boys, wanting them to enter the worlds of medicine or law in particular, but were initially quite happy for their daughters to leave school at sixteen and stack shelves in the local supermarket as a limit on their ambition.

As a staff, we managed to convince some of them to revise their opinions but others remained unconvinced and clung to their long established beliefs.

With occasional minor modifications they all wore the same uniforms and participated in the daily school assembly, singing the hymns and saying the prayers.

Several of them excelled on the games field and many of them were record-breakers, their sporting prowess instrumental in helping them to settle in and become very much part of the school scene. Ayub Khalid, was a natural athlete who loved every minute of his time competing on the track and in the field events.

None seemed to faze him and he would have entered everything if he had been allowed.

"Are You Strong, Lass?"

He was a big, strong lad with an athletic build and he looked much older than his thirteen years.

The other boys in the year group were envious of his honed physique and impressed by his facial hair.

Dusty Miller, the PE teacher, quickly recognised his talent and spent hours giving him extra coaching and encouraging him to follow his sporting dreams.

Humour, intentional or otherwise, played a big part in making school life tolerable for both the kids and staff.

As a young and very inexperienced female teacher I was fair game for a lot of the adolescent lads and their innuendo and I have to admit being rather flattered by it and quite happy to blush.

Very early on, I was making my way to my classroom at the end of break weaving my way carefully through groups of hormonal teenage boys who were draped everywhere and reluctant to go to class.

As I tried to ease my way past one gang, a hidden voice rang out to the captive audience, "I dreamed about you last night, Miss."

"Did you?" I replied, a little flustered.

"No, you wouldn't let me!" came the quick-fire reply which was greeted by a cacophony of raucous laughter as I scurried off to classroom sanctuary as quickly as my stiletto heels would allow me.

There was a huge Police Training Academy situated not too far away from school and I was convinced that several of their new recruits learned to cut their teeth on us and made us an integral part of their learning programme.

These were no visits to foster community relations or pass on the delights of Tufty the squirrel or the green cross code or to oversee cycling proficiency tests.

Most likely it was investigations and interviews into

items that had gone missing from various locations, which were numerous and long.

I remember my lessons being interrupted on occasions by the school secretary to request some miscreant's presence in the headmaster's office.

There were no telephone links to the various parts of the school in those days, so the poor lady spent much of her time walking the not inconsiderable distances between her work station and the classrooms.

She kept a pair of 'flatties' next to her desk specifically for that purpose.

If he deemed it serious enough, occasionally the head went searching for the purported culprit himself; we all knew then that the accusations were major.

Penknives, bottles of Magnet Pale Ale, rucksacks, transistor radios and various technical gadgets, lead piping and Timex watches were among the list of missing items on a regular basis and chief suspects eminently predictable, often with a family history for such behaviour.

They were interrogated at length in offices and classrooms, the police were very well acquainted with those involved and many a scam thwarted.

The police also attended to investigate missing pupils and runaways.

A number of our kids had problems at home and felt that the only way of coping was to leave and, hearing some of their tales of hardship, deprivation and worse, it was easy to see why.

The evidence of physical and mental abuse on a regular basis was never far from the surface.

The constables consistently handled it well and sensitively and occasionally I had to attend case reviews arranged by the local authority and listen to the professionals giving their advice and recommendations. In those idealistic days post-graduation, it was a terrifying listen.

I didn't feel as though I could contribute much but I watched and learned the causes, process and outcomes and decided very early on that a teacher's job was to be on the child's side, to fight for the ones who had no voice and to try and ensure that some sort of justice was done to limit the damage.

The police would also try and sort out the disagreements and feuds which flared up from time to time on the estate.

Families frequently had old scores to settle and the kids were often caught up in the middle, the boys in blue intervening in an effort to keep the peace or take out the sting. Whenever in school, their presence certainly became a spectator sport.

One chilly September evening on the estate, Bolton Road became the battleground for a notorious exchange.

The Cooper and Bayston families had decided to escalate a long running feud with multiple members outside trading threatening insults.

Apparently, Mrs Bayston had been happy to do a bit of knitting for Mrs Cooper who was expecting a baby at the end of the month but a chance remark down the laundrette had made Mrs Bayston rethink.

She had been minding her own business, trying to keep warm in the far corner having run out of coins to feed the electric meter at home, when she heard two women mention her husband's name.

Pricking her ears up and lifting her eyes from the torn *Woman's Weekly* she had found on the floor, she quickly got the gist of the conversation.

"Steve Bayston, that bloke who works at the railway

190

station. It's 'im that knocked up that Mrs Cooper, who's our Trish's boss at the café, you wouldn't have thought he had it in him," she heard being stage-whispered.

The showdown was set and over nine days the accusations flew over the respective doorsteps as the crowd witnessing it became ever greater – it was like having their own, personal episode of *Coronation Street*.

It all blew over eventually but the matinee jacket remained unknitted and one can only speculate where the needles ended up.

Teenage pregnancies were a fact of life in school, no matter what the discussions about the 'facts of life.'

All the lessons were in place but had mainly been giggled through, the relevant literature posted in school and occasional extra talks given about the implications, but inevitably for some, to no avail.

I could never get really angry with the girls because I felt they were the victims in the situation.

They often had few, if any, positive role models to help and advise them nor access to magazines like *Jackie* and their problem pages.

Some of them felt that getting pregnant would afford them the attention they craved even if they hadn't planned it that way or understood the accompanying responsibilities.

The outcome tended to be as a result of something spontaneous so contraceptives were not high on the agenda for either party.

They mistakenly thought a baby would be an escape, something for them to love and, perhaps, be loved in return.

One of the girls was devastated to give birth to a stillborn baby. She was sixteen and, in so many ways, still a baby herself really and she cried uncontrollably as I tried to comfort her.

She had already split up with her boyfriend who had moved on to pastures new and she was terrified that her parents would throw her out because she couldn't do anything right. We did all we could to help her come to terms and get through it.

Conversely, Jane was so pleased and excited to give birth to a bouncing baby boy with a shock of ginger hair and took great pride in showing me that she could achieve something. To her it was her rite of passage and we were on a par; she was a real woman.

Too often, however, the girls didn't learn from the unexpected experience, continued to be reckless in their choices and became saddled before they had even had a chance to live their lives.

Dear Mr and Mrs Davis,

I am sorry to have to be writing to you so soon after my last letter but Kenneth was again caught stealing from the general store on Starling Road. The owner has been up to school and regrettably he is considering banning all school pupils from the shop.

He has asked me to arrange a meeting with the school and yourselves to see if anything can be resolved as he is most reluctant to get the police involved. He is a very reasonable man and I am most anxious to support him as best I can.

I am sure that you are aware of the seriousness of the situation and also of, the necessity to try and point out the error of his ways to Kenneth before it is too late.

I should be grateful if you would either telephone the school or call at your earliest convenience to make an appointment with the school secretary.

Yours sincerely,
Stanley Cowburn, Headmaster

15.

Yorkshire Days

Dear Mr and Mrs Kosavecic,

As you will know, Vaso was the outstanding athlete yesterday at sports day and it has now been confirmed that he broke two school records, in the under 14 high jump and the junior sprint. You must be very proud of him and justifiably so. The school has been in touch with the local press and they would like to come to school tomorrow afternoon to take a photograph and write an article about him.

We would very much like you to be there as well if at all possible if your work shift patterns allow.

Please telephone my secretary to let her know if you are able to. I very much hope that you will be able to share in this very proud occasion with your son.

Yours sincerely,
Stanley Cowburn,
Headmaster

"Are You Strong, Lass?"

FOR my very first school sports day in 1970, soon after I joined, the weather was kind and pleasantly warm for what, for some pupils, was the most important date in the school calendar.

The stage was theirs and what, perhaps, they lacked in academic ability could be made up for on their preferred level playing field, to show both their classmates and teachers what they could really do.

They strutted about like peacocks and enjoyed and basked in the unprecedented and rare positive attention deservedly afforded to them.

I wasn't quite sure what exactly to expect being fresh out of graduate training.

We had discussed the plan of action for the day at a staff meeting and there had been various missives sent round along with a long list of allocated jobs for the day itself.

This had been drawn up by the PE staff and seemed to cause great consternation among nearly everyone who was to be involved.

A few of the teachers wanted to avoid being stationed too near to particular parents or members of the PTA, others had traded duties the previous year for hope of a cushier number this time but such promises had been seemingly forgotten, and no-one wanted toilet duty or patrolling the grounds for those who had sneaked off for a smoke, which meant they didn't see any of the events.

I listened in naive wonderment and with some trepidation at the exchanges, fearing that with special games as part of my qualification, I might get asked to do something vital before I'd had chance to properly learn the ropes.

As it turned out, I was drafted into helping one of the more senior lady teachers control the masses who were due to watch from the grass banking surrounding the track and field.

The heats for most of the athletic events had been held during games lessons the previous week with varying degrees of proficiency.

High jump, hop, skip and jump, long jump and, somewhat scarily, javelin constituted the field events, and the 100 yards, 220 and 880 races were the mainstays on the track.

All were eagerly contested to try and relay practices were held at dinner time, with the house captains and members of staff shouting encouragement and advice, and the older pupils coaching the younger ones.

Not all who were seconded into trying out were happy at the prospect and some of the disaffected tried to disrupt proceedings for the others but the overall sense was of camaraderie and teamwork and the events leading up to and on the day extremely well organised.

The kids wore simple PE kit if their parents could afford it and they remembered to bring it. The majority had plain black plimsolls or pumps many of which were borrowed – occasionally without permission – or hand me downs and didn't fit properly, which made their feats all the more admirable.

There was a very accurate system of record keeping so that children could compare themselves and their achievements with alumni and competition was very much encouraged and deemed to be desirable.

The school notice boards boasted past successes and listed the school athletic records which were constantly scrutinised by those who thought that they were in with a real chance of breaking them.

Parents were welcome on the day to cheer their offspring on but attendance wasn't expected.

"Are You Strong, Lass?"

In the fortnight between the heats and sports day finals, the teaching staff had a greater job in holding attention for those who dreamed of being the latest Lillian Board or Bob Beamon.

They were often caught wistfully looking at the window planning their personal bests and victory salutes, accepting the adulation and glory.

Come our version of the Olympics, and the usual timetable carried on in the morning, several of the most fancied athletes often late as they were in serious preparation and chose a lie in over lessons. After registration in the afternoon, the competitors went to one holding station and the spectators another, as the excitement and inevitable good-natured high spirits increased.

I made my way tentatively to find Mrs Silver and we took up our designated post. She was an old hand who stood no nonsense either inside or outside the classroom.

"Whatever they say to you, however hard they plead, whatever faces they pull, under no circumstances allow them to leave the banking!" she boomed at me from inside a green nylon tracksuit she borrowed from her husband every year and which was about two sizes too small, to evident but muted amusement from all.

"They will all have had the opportunity to go to the toilet before we get out there and, as far as I am aware, nobody has a medical note about a weak bladder. And even if they do produce one, do not let them go off the banking!

"They will try it on, crossing their legs and squealing with pretend pain, but it is all a lot of nonsense and we are not having it! I repeat, do not let them off the banking!"

I was left in no doubt as to my instructions and, in the main, on our side of the bank, we did not have any such nonsense.

I didn't get to do much event watching except for the final relay but I did enjoy it and the atmosphere in general.

The parents who came sat enthralled and captivated as their young ones took centre stage.

Before the event came to a formal end, trophies and medals were presented and the winning house announced to an increasingly raucous gathering and amid much cheering.

Warren House were the victors that day, green ribbons were tied to the cup and everyone, whether they had participated or not, joining in with the reflected glory as the joint captains lifted it skywards.

The following day saw the notice boards in the main corridor refreshed with beautifully crafted lists – done by the immaculate hand of the geography teacher – of winners, record breakers and their times, much to the delight of the assembled who gathered round it noisily.

The new heroes and heroines of the hour were cheered and acknowledged and there was a real sense of achievement in school for several days afterwards.

Another important day in the sporting calendar was, unquestionably, the fixtures when the staff challenged the pupils.

Depending on weather and schedules they could be one a term but, in most sports, it was an annual grudge match.

I'd played in them as a pupil back in Otley and the kids couldn't wait to get legally stuck in to their supposed betters, the protégés upstaging the masters.

Hockey, football and rounders were the favourites and, as I remember, the teams were sometimes mixed to even the outcome.

Mrs Silver, her ample proportions squashed into a pair of divided navy blue shorts and her aertex blouse stretched perilously tight over her ample bosom, was frequently seen speeding down the wing, hockey stick in hand with a steely determination in her eyes as she flicked the ball adroitly to the centre forward.

Overall the matches were played out in a positive and good-natured spirit that benefitted all, the entire school allowed out to watch the drama unfold.

The pupils who had been selected were cheered fervently every time they outwitted the common enemy.

If they scored a goal, a huge roar would go up, as it would if teachers fell over or found themselves in compromising and embarrassing positions.

When the final whistle was blown, after what seemed like an eternity to the staff, cheers were sounded regardless of a result that was always announced in assembly the following day and recorded on the sports notice boards for posterity and finger pointing.

The real sport for the majority of the spectators had been the cheering, jeering and occasional leering for that magic hour when they were free of the constraints of the classroom and could see the teachers in a very different light.

The words I feared hearing the most were, "Isn't it your duty day today?"

A list was posted on the staffroom notice board which gave you your designated day and duty area, and then it was down to you.

You had to be ready for anything and you had to develop a tough outer shell to deal with it all and still emerge relatively unscathed.

I was fortunate to be given good advice by senior colleagues at the outset, which clarified certain issues and highlighted potential pitfalls.

The rota covered break and dinner time and duties

were shared with at least one other colleague with one inside and the other outside.

Usually the most senior colleague made the choice which varied as both carried their inherent dangers.

Whatever the weather, large numbers wanted to stay in and that was seen to be the most challenging area and the one I seemed to be lumbered with the most. It saw me patrolling the corridors trying to establish an air of authority although that pretence was quickly stripped away.

I was supposed to be sniffing out miscreants who were lurking in classrooms, often trying to keep warm.

The majority were girls who, more often than not just wanted to gossip, talk about make-up and boys.

I tended to turn a blind eye to some of their pleadings whilst letting them know I had cut them some slack in the hope that at some stage the favour would be repaid. I saw it as part of the getting to know you process.

Boys preferred massing outside, often in inappropriate clothes just to prove how hard they were.

Duties were also about establishing a line, especially if you were a novice.

Jonathan Ferris was definitely not an insider and when I encountered him in the first floor geography room with a small, select group of his pals, I was rather taken by surprise.

He was sprawled like a stick insect over the desk, his thin legs dangling and swinging precariously.

"Come on now, Jonathan, you know you shouldn't be in here at break time. Outside please, all of you now," I said, summoning up courage.

"Why should we? Just feel like staying in today. And I 'aven't got mi big woolly jumper. Had to lend it to our Ian cos he has a right bad cold," he responded to see how far he could push his luck.

"Rules are rules. We can't just break them when we feel like it. Life's not like that. Come on, I shan't tell you again," I replied but without real authority in my voice.

"Well other folk do and our lass reckons that rules are only there to be broken," he said testing my patience and influence.

"I'm going to count to ten and if you are still in this room by then then I shall refer you all to Mr Forbes."

The others looked at me and then at Jonathan and then at me again. I walked slowly towards the group, trying to look as fierce as I could but feeling the exact opposite and began countdown.

Walking towards them as I did, we were almost face to face as I got to one, at which point they all moved towards the window and, one by one, proceeded to jump out.

I was taken aback, I'd won the battle but they'd had the last laugh, and I sat down and wondered if I'd handled it well, having got the desired result, or been made to look a fool. Fortunately, although it was a fair drop to the playground below, they were all uninjured and had obviously done it before but I hadn't known that as I peered gingerly through the glass fearful of possible carnage on the tarmac below.

They'd run off laughing at their triumph and, once duty finished, I tentatively went back to the staffroom expecting it to be the topic of conversation and to be sent for by the head but nobody mentioned it – it was as if such exploits were totally normal.

The twenty minute slots seemed to last an eternity whilst I got used to them and most of mine initially seemed to fall on a Monday, the most uncooperative day of the week.

The most likely area of dissent and potential confrontation outside were the dreaded bike sheds.

A significant number of the boys cycled to school and parked their wheels in the bike racks.

Bikes were a big part in a teenage boy's life and there was one in particular which they all longed to own, the Raleigh Chopper.

Five speed Sturmey Archer gears fitted on the frame and not the handlebars, a kickstand, long padded high back seat, differently sized wheels encased in bobbed mudguards and high-rise handlebars, it was coveted above all others.

The sheds were a good place to congregate and exchange the latest gossip, tell dirty jokes, swap comics, compare the latest stickers, swap cards that their Nan had given them from inside the PG Tips box and generally hang out.

Open and spaciously laid out, they were deemed to be out of bounds at break and dinner times because they were positioned at the front of the school and away from the main playground area in the somewhat sprawling site and so difficult to police.

That only served to make them a more attractive proposition for those who wanted to test the boundaries.

It was worse when the decision was made to 'leave the bell off.'

If the weather was deemed to be fine and warm enough, then the cry would go up in the staffroom, and Miss D.M. Brooke would be persuaded to go along with the plan to extend break.

A child would then be dispatched to convey the news to the poor member of staff on duty and as those back at base settled back to check the racing tips or brew another cuppa, the poor sap trying to maintain order had their torment near doubled.

When the call went out, the bike sheds became the

meeting point of choice for many outside so as to try and sneak an extra, illicit fag for some; inside it was the crammed toilets and, most often, the teacher's extra breathing space was deemed preferable on a Monday.

Some of the girls loved the toilets and even viewed them as their second home. This was the place where important decisions were made and their world put to rights.

There was an unwritten hierarchical order which was rigidly adhered to, and which determined where everyone sat and held court, younger girls accepting their allotted place in the pecking order and corner, hoping that the crown would pass to them one day.

With the smell of Parma Violets permeating, they would also enjoy exchanging cosmetics items, which they were not supposed to have in school, and compare and contrast their respective and most recent romantic liaisons.

Who had managed to get past 'first base'? Who had reached number five, panicked and got cold feet and who'd actually gone all the way?

The size and intensity of recently acquired love bites was always a hot topic of conversation and they would enjoy sharing tips with each other as to the best way of concealing them.

They'd also use the facilities as a café and sit on the floor gorging themselves on penny Fruit Salad and Black Jack chews, their tongues turning orange or black as the discussions got more animated.

All of that was manageable for the duty teacher, but the difficulty was smoking and the toilets was deemed to be safe ground. When caught, some of them would put up a valiant fight before extinguishing them and try to persuade you to let them finish it with one last, long drag, claiming it was all that got them through the day.

It also brought a certain cachet among the group to be the provider.

The other major issue was stopping the boys trying to get into the girls' toilets and I still shudder at the first time I found opposite sexes in the same cubicle.

It was all I could do to conjure up my most disapproving look and plead with them to relinquish their adolescent lust, readjust their clothing, wash their hands and move along to lessons as quickly as they could.

They never showed the slightest hint of embarrassment having been compromised either.

One of the boys who I had caught tended to view the whole episode as a badge of honour and confided in me shortly afterwards that he viewed it as part of his education, a practical biology lesson.

Discovering such dangerous liaisons certainly gave me a fund of shocking tales with which to regale colleagues in the safe haven of the staffroom, once the dreaded duty was over.

Dear Miss,

That packet of Woodbines that you took off our Philip last week, we need it back now.

He should never have taken them to school in the first place and they don't even belong to him. They are his grandpa's and I can tell you that he is not best suited having to do without them.

So, let us have them back, please, and we'll say no more about it. Much thanks.

Sharon Copeland (mother)

16.

Yorkshire Post

Dear Mrs Padgett,

Our Sarah has just told us that you are leaving at the end of this term and moving to another school in the area.

We would just like to thank you for all the advice you have given her during her time there and, in particular, for helping her through the odd difficult patch which she has experienced.

Her older brother and sister also remember you with great affection and wish you well in your new job.

Sarah has a small present for you in her bag which we hope you will accept with our very best wishes for the future.

Good luck and thank you again.

Yours sincerely,
Freda and Arthur Macmillan

Dear Mr and Mrs Macmillan,

I was very touched by your kind words and good wishes. Letters like yours make the job even more worthwhile and I am only pleased that I was able to play a small part in Sarah's educational journey.

I'm sure that she will continue to make good progress with her studies and I have told her that I know she can deal with most situations now that she has overcome her demons. Please remember me to Ruth and Mark as well.

I shall treasure Sarah's present and place it in a prominent position on my new desk. It will serve as a constant reminder to me as to what we can all achieve when we work together. I suppose that is what teaching is all about, really.

I feel very privileged to have worked at this school and I like to think that I have been there for my pupils and made a small difference.

I hope that Sarah finds a job in which she is both happy and fulfilled; I know how lucky I've been in that regard.

I've met some wonderful pupils and parents here and I shall take away very many happy memories.

In the words of my French master at grammar school in the 1960s; 'Find a job that you really love and you'll never work again.'

Yours sincerely,
Kathryn Padgett

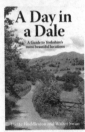

The Barefoot Shepherdess

and Women of the Dales

By Yvette Huddleston & Walter Swan

T*he Barefoot Shepherdess and Women of the Dales* celebrates the variety and versatility of a dozen or more determined women who have made a distinctive life for themselves 'far from the madding crowd'.

The Yorkshire Dales attracts tourists aplenty to appreciate the beauties of the local landscape but most visitors return to their towns and cities, renewed by the peace and quiet of the countryside, though unable to leave their modern, urban lifestyle for too long.

Women like Alison O'Neill, who owns her own flock of sheep and designs her own brand of tweed clothing, demonstrate that you can live a life of independence and fulfilment even in Britain's remotest regions. There are inevitable hardships to be endured but innumerable compensations when the Dales are on your doorstep.

Each chapter features inspirational women who have made the choice to live and work collaboratively with the people and places of the Yorkshire landscape. What they have in common - farmers, artists, vets, publicans, entrepreneurs, artisans, academics, curators and vicars - is a passion for life where Yorkshire countryside and community coincide.

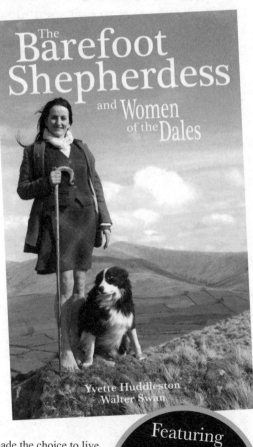

Featuring personalities from the ITV series **The Dales**

Investigate our other titles and
stay up to date with all our latest releases at
www.scratchingshedpublishing.co.uk